The Writer's Grammar Guide

EASY GROUND RULES
FOR SUCCESSFUL WRITTEN ENGLISH

Jane Walpole

A FIRESIDE BOOK
Published by Simon & Schuster, Inc.
NEW YORK

Copyright © 1980 by Jane Walpole
All rights reserved
including the right of reproduction
in whole or in part in any form

First Fireside Edition, 1984
Published by Simon & Schuster, Inc.
Simon & Schuster Building
Rockefeller Center
1230 Avenue of the Americas
New York, New York 10020

FIRESIDE and colophon are registered trademarks of Simon & Schuster, Inc.
Editorial/production supervision and interior design by Eric Newman
Manufacturing buyer: Cathie Lenard
Manufactured in the United States of America

3 5 7 9 10 8 6 4 2 Pbk.

Library of Congress Cataloging in Publication Data

Walpole, Jane.
  The writer's grammar guide.

  Originally published: A writer's guide. Englewood
Cliffs, N.J.: Prentice-Hall, c1980.
  Includes index.
  1. English language—Rhetoric. 2. English language
—Grammar—1950–   . I. Title.
PE1408.W31323   1984   428'.2   84-10341
ISBN 0-671-53046-1 Pbk.

Contents

Preface

"You teach English? Oh, oh—I'd better watch my grammar."

This introductory quip goes with the territory. English teachers have learned to force a smile and try to keep the conversation alive. Behind the defensive joke, though, lies a spontaneous gut equation: English = grammar. And too often, grammar = guilt.

Many adults, otherwise well educated, articulate, and successful in their lives, feel queasy about grammar. They know it has something to do with nouns and verbs, and they know they've never learned it—probably because they were never really taught it. Now it seems to be too late. They find grammar texts written for students needing basic remediation, inching along step by tiny step. They find grammar handbooks written for the initiated, explaining the finer points of the game to those who already know the players. So the educated adult remains trapped in uneasy ignorance.

Some English teachers cheerily assert that grammar doesn't matter. Most professionals know better. Journalism classes bog down with students who can't write a straight sentence. Law schools struggle with students whose prose would baffle Blackstone. Engineering students can't prepare clear specifications.

Graduate students write dissertations that choke in tangled syntax. Business offices mire down in muddy memos. And everyone knows that government means gobbledygook.

Grammar does indeed matter. It is an integral piece of man's unique talent—language. The ability to use grammar is as much a part of each person as the ability to breathe. True, we can talk or write—that is, use grammar—without knowing the anatomy of a sentence. We can also breathe without knowing what our lungs are or how they work. But knowledge is enlightening. If we understand how sentences work, we are better able to write precisely and effectively. A familiarity with grammar can lessen the paralyzing fear of error, so that we can use our language with confidence.

Grammar also makes sense. This book explains the larger concepts of grammar as a framework for the smaller details. It shows you how the parts of a sentence fit together logically to operate in an intelligible statement and how those parts can be rearranged to give variety and style to your writing. As you read it, you will begin to understand the grammar that you've been using most of your life. Best of all, your guilt will melt away. You may continue to "watch your grammar," but only because it is a fascinating thing to watch.

A Writer's Guide

I

What This Book Is All About

1

You and This Book

Perhaps you are an engineer or a business executive whose livelihood depends on producing well-written reports. As you organize your ideas, you find yourself stumbling over questions of grammar. Perhaps you are a graduate student, in your seventh year of university work. As you prepare the dissertation upon which your academic reputation hinges, you too may come face to face with grammatical bugbears.

Or you may be an upperclassman who whizzed through freshman comp but whose term papers are now returned red-inked from grammar errors. Or a secretary who must disentangle your boss's sentences. Or a parent overseeing your child's homework. Or a doctor preparing a paper for a medical journal. Whoever you are, if your activities—professional, academic, or personal—require an ability to write correctly, and if your last formal grammar training has left you unsure of the difference between a predicate nominative and a nominative absolute, this book is designed to help you.

It is not a complete grammar of the English language. It is not a grammar handbook for quick reference to forms and terms. In fact, you will see neither *predicate nominative* nor

3

nominative absolute defined in these pages. The Latinate terms are not important when you write a paper.

What this book does offer you is a survey of the essential grammar needed by a writer. It attempts, moreover, to present this survey in a perspective that illuminates the rationale and logic of grammar. For, despite what your experience might suggest, grammar is not an arbitrary maze of rules concocted to trip you up. Grammar is a reflection of the way the human mind thinks and speaks. Written grammar (that is, the grammar that writers rather than speakers use) represents the clearest way to transmit thoughts from the writer's mind to the reader's through the medium of words, paper, and ink. A clear thought is a logical thought, and written grammar encapsulates that logic.

More specifically, what this book offers is a survey broken into eight sections. After a brief examination of the nature of grammar, you'll meet some of the terms used to discuss sentences. Then comes a look at the independent clause, the basic unit of all written thought. Punctuation is next—the special punctuation that reflects grammatical patterns. After you read about writing and punctuating single sentences, you'll find a section on creating bigger sentences, then another one on creating <u>better</u> sentences in polished prose that hangs together smoothly. Unfortunately, grammar has its sticky pitfalls, and the next section looks at some of these problem areas. Finally, a brief epilogue leads you from the confines of a grammatical sentence to the wider fields of real writing.

This book is as concise as its subject permits. To get the most benefit from it, you should read it from cover to cover, because its ideas build cumulatively. Once you are familiar with its contents, you might want to use it as a handy reference. But after you have absorbed its lessons, you may feel so relaxed and reassured about grammatical problems that you will have few occasions to consult it. If you don't need to use this book again, it will have served its purpose well.

2

Grammar
and Writing

Two questions need to be explored at the outset. First, what precisely is "grammar"? Next, why is this book limited to written grammar? That is, does written grammar differ from spoken grammar? And if so, in what ways?

Let's begin with a definition of grammar—or, actually, three definitions. To start with, *grammar* refers to the way a language works as it translates ideas inside someone's mind into spoken sounds. Certain sounds are arbitrarily connected with certain "real" things or referents; these sounds we call *words*. Then the words are strung together in specific patterns or structures that can be re-translated by another mind back into ideas—ideas that should more or less resemble the original ideas. Thus, language can be defined as sounds articulated according to the rules of grammar, and through language we are able to transmit ideas from one mind to another. Looked at this way, the rules of grammar closely reproduce the thought processes of the human brain—which is scarcely surprising, since the human brain devised language and its grammar in the first place.

Many scholars who study languages have attempted to formulate the basic patterns of grammar into a coherent set of

5

rules. This gives us a second definition of *grammar:* a system for classifying and describing the grammatical features of a given language. These systems are artificial models designed to mirror as accurately as possible the natural workings of a language. Here we are only interested in models that describe the grammar of the English language, and we could find many to choose from. There is the traditional model of grammar that you probably studied in school, but there are also newer systems, like structural linguistics, transformational grammar, case grammar, stratificational grammar, and tagmemics. This book follows fairly traditional lines, but it's worth knowing that "grammar" is not a single, inflexible system. Any number of grammar systems have been devised to describe and discuss the same phenomenon, the actual grammar that we demonstrate when we use the English language.

Finally, the word *grammar* is applied to a given kind of book, one that talks about language use (the first meaning of *grammar*), based on some specific model (the second meaning). These grammars range from simple texts for fifth-graders to complex volumes for linguists, and from sequential drills to alphabetized reference guides. This book, then, is a grammar in the third sense of the word—a book, more specifically, that talks about the grammar you call into play when you write.

But why a grammar for <u>writers</u>? The answer lies in the differences between speech and writing. Basic important similarities exist, of course, but the differences are what we are interested in. The divergence stems, obviously enough, from the two ways of producing language. Speech consists of organized and segmented noise; it leaves the speaker's mouth, rattles on the listener's eardrums, and dissipates, gone forever. Writing consists of organized and segmented marks on paper; it hits the reader's eye once, twice, as often as need be, without disappearing. So writing has requirements that speech lacks (just as speech has special requirements, although we are not interested in them here).

For one thing, writing involves spelling, building the correct forms for words. And word forms are part of grammar. As a case in point, you need to <u>write</u> *bear* and *bare* in different forms, but you <u>speak</u> them the same.

For another thing, writing requires that you create a context for your ideas and explain those ideas as clearly and precisely as seems necessary to establish communication with your reader. In talking, your context surrounds you and your listener. You can point your finger and say, with perfect clarity, "There it is." In writing, though, you'd need to explain where *there* is and what *it* is—and these explanations involve grammar.

Writing also permits you to use more complicated sentence patterns than might appear in speech. This means that you can attain greater precision of thought, shading a point here, adding an example there, getting just the right relationship between ideas as you strive toward the ideal: communication with no possibility of misunderstanding. In speech, we tend to use rather simple grammatical patterns, for they are adequate to most occasions. Indeed, at times a grunt says as much as a complete sentence. But in writing, we have need of more choices. We can choose the simple sentence. On the other hand, we can go to any length and complexity we wish in order to present an idea effectively. As an example of written grammar, consider the opening sentence of the Declaration of Independence:

> When, in the course of human events, it becomes necessary for one people to dissolve the political bands which have connected them with another, and to assume, among the powers of the earth, the separate and equal station to which the laws of nature and of nature's God entitle them, a decent respect to the opinions of mankind requires that they should declare the causes which impel them to the separation.

No one would ever speak this sentence. But for its purpose, to project dignity and solemnity, its complex written grammar still rings impressively across the ages.

And this brings us to the next distinguishing feature we need to note about written grammar. Any piece of writing intended for another's eyes is a permanent record, if not "for the ages," at least for repeated readings. Thus, a knowledge of acceptable grammar becomes a face-saver, because if you write a grammatical goof, it remains an embarrassment on the paper for as long as it's read. An occasional spoken error gets washed away in the stream of words, or you can back up and start the sentence again. But a written error just sits there. At best, your reader understands what you meant and merely thinks a tad less highly of you. At worst, the bad grammar so garbles your sentence and your ideas that your reader can get no meaning from the sentence at all or (perhaps more dangerous) guesses at the wrong meaning. The pains that you take to assure clear, smooth grammar pay off in the ease and pleasure that your reader experiences in comprehending you. And if your reader can understand your writing, you have a better chance of getting your ideas accepted. So though the first beneficiary of good grammar is the reader, in the long run the beneficiary is the writer—you.

Luckily, there is one other saving difference between speech and writing. Speech is spontaneous; writing is deliberate. We usually blurt out our words without too much conscious preliminary thought on how they should be arranged. (In fact, except for prepared statements, we are seldom aware of <u>any</u> conscious thought. Yet most of our utterances are clear and meaningful. How we manage this trick is one of the greatest miracles and mysteries of man.) In contrast, writing lacks the urgency of speech. If we wish to take the time to write well, the time is normally available to us. So we can think, add, change, delete, rearrange, do whatever we choose, in order to frame our written sentences as correctly and effectively as possible. Without the redeeming grace period that writing affords us, most of us would throw in our pens.

All in all, written language is in so many significant respects distinct from spoken language that some linguists look upon it as a separate dialect, one that no one speaks but every literate person writes. If you've ever met the uncomfortably pompous kind of person who "talks like a book," you know what it sounds like to <u>speak</u> written English in ordinary conversation. It just doesn't sound natural. Good prose does approximate good, careful, intelligent speech, in that it can be read aloud easily and gracefully. But carefully written language represents a unique dialect shared by anyone who has learned the trick of writing well.

Spoken dialects can vary widely from region to region or from social class to social class. As a simple example, look at the word *vase.* In different spoken dialects it might be pronounced to rhyme with *face* or *faze* or *Oz.* But in writing, it has to be *v-a-s-e.* Or in some dialects, the plural *-s* is dropped in speaking a sentence like *He drove three mile to work.* But in writing, the *-s* must appear on *miles,* for written English is far more standardized than speech. Indeed, the acceptable written form of the language is often referred to as Standard Written English.

Some people have condemned Standard Written English as an elitist dialect used to sort out sheep from goats. It is true that the dialect operates only within a closed circle of communicants. But the sole requirement for entry into the circle is education, and education is open to all who choose to learn. No matter what spoken-dialect community these educated persons belong to, no matter how divergent their personal speech patterns, no matter even if English is their first language or an acquired one, when they write careful prose, they all use the same general dialect—a Standard Written English obliterating geographic, racial, and socioeconomic distinctions. Lin Yu-tang, Winston Churchill, and Eldridge Cleaver may have shared little else, but they all shared the same written language. So welcome to the circle. You are in good company.

3

Grammar, Usage, and Mechanics

Before getting into grammar, we must try to separate three distinct but overlapping aspects of language: grammar, usage, and mechanics.

Within the narrow purposes of this book, **grammar** refers to the forms, structures, and functions of written English only. We shall return to this definition later and discuss its terms in detail. But briefly, it means that certain forms of words are put together to build certain structures according to certain rules and patterns (rules that really exist in the language, not rules that someone made up). These words and structures then function in definite ways within larger structures. For example, certain word forms go together to build the structure of a prepositional phrase, and that small structure may function as a noun modifier within a larger structure, such as a clause. At the heart of grammar, then, are form, structure, and function.

Usage goes beyond grammar to examine the acceptability or the appropriateness of certain words or phrases in certain situations. Should you say *It is I* or *It is me*? *Everyone has his book* or *Everyone has their books*? *Between* or *among*? *Different from* or *different than*? If you <u>may</u> use some of these forms, where and when are they acceptable? Questions like these are not, strictly speaking, matters of grammar, although they often impinge on grammar. Their answers depend on the usage of recognized and respected practitioners of the English language.

Grammar and usage share a gray borderline. Straddling this line are problems of "agreement," or joint characteristics, between words. A singular subject must be joined with a singular verb. A given pronoun must be feminine in order to agree with the feminine noun it replaces. Most systematized rules of grammar demand these and other points of agreement, which can become rather complicated. But usage may be less demanding. A strict adherence to grammar rules requires *It is I* as the only proper form. Yet we all hear (and many of us say) *It's me*. Usage—that is, actual practice—seems to contradict grammar. On closer examination, though, we learn that usage merely <u>extends</u> grammar, adjusting its rules to meet differing circumstances.

Usage choices, for example, may often vary between speech and writing. In speech, *It's me* is almost always the preferred form. Someone identifying a figure in a snapshot would probably (and rightly) say, *That's him*. Writing, however, is usually more conservative than speech. You should always <u>write</u> *It is I* or *That is he*—unless you are reproducing a conversational style. Fortunately, the occasion to write *It is I* rarely arises. Suppose, though, you are preparing a paper on Jonas Salk. You might write, *It was he who first developed a polio vaccine. He* may sound formal, but in this context you would be aiming at formality.

Written usage varies with the level of formality of your paper, and also with its purpose: to be serious, humorous, relaxed, official, or what you will. Slang and contractions, for instance, may be appropriate in some informal writing but would normally be quite out of place in a professional report. So usage depends on circumstances. You need a sensitivity to language for choosing the right words, a sensitivity gained through long exposure to speech and reading. Some situations, though, require expert guidance. This book will offer a few tips on usage, especially in that murky area of agreement. But for more thorough information, you should consult one of the many good dictionaries of usage, such as those mentioned in Chapter 34. You'll find useful—and sometimes surprising—advice in them, so check them out.

Mechanics deals with the picky points of writing: spelling, for example, or capitalization, abbreviations, certain punctuation conventions—all the apparently trivial yet important rules of writing etiquette that a careful person observes. Again, questions of mechanics often get mixed in with both grammar and usage. Is an apostrophe a grammatical mark of possession and contraction? Or is it a mechanical requirement? Is the choice between *Ph.D.* and *PhD* a matter of mechanics or of usage? The dividing lines are fuzzy, but it's better to try to sort mechanics out separately. Any number of English handbooks have a section on mechanics, and several books listed in Chapter 34 provide detailed coverage of mechanics conventions. It's wiser to consult such books and be right than to guess and be sorry.

Because usage and mechanics cannot always be neatly dissevered from grammar, this book will on occasion make a few comments on usage, and fewer still on mechanics. For the most part, though, it will focus on grammar—the forms, structures, and functions that a writer needs to know.

II

How to Talk About Grammar

4

Some
Preliminary Concepts

Every specialized activity has its own jargon, terms which permit the initiated to discuss that activity with precision and clarity. Grammar is no exception. Although the terms used in this book have been kept to a minimum, you need to be familiar with them in order to understand how language works. In fact, you probably are already acquainted with them, but only in a vague, misty fashion. If you are like most adults, you no doubt feel you've forgotten all the grammar you ever knew.

Not so! Here is a point that needs to be stressed. Right now you know more grammar than you know you know. You may not know the <u>terms</u>, so you have trouble talking about grammar—textbook grammar, that is. But because you can speak and read English, you do know English grammar—the important grammar of how to use language.

Therefore, value your own instincts. Trust your own ear. At least 90 percent of the time, what <u>sounds</u> good will be good grammar. Writing is not speech put on paper. You should seldom try to "write the way you speak," and anyone who gives you this advice is misleading you. But good writing <u>is</u> speakable. That is, good writing read aloud should reflect the pauses, pitches, nuances, and rhythms of the human voice. So read your

"I used to know all about verbs, nouns, and pronouns,
but that was long, long ago."

Drawing by Ross; © 1979
The New Yorker Magazine, Inc.

work aloud as if you were addressing an audience, slowly and with proper emphasis. And <u>listen</u> to what you have written.

If your voice moves smoothly and naturally through the words, you have probably written both correctly and effectively. If your tongue stumbles, if you have to back up and re-start a sentence, if your writing sounds awkward, you may have problems. <u>Speaking</u> your writing is the best method for pin-pointing grammatical bobbles and stylistic gaffes. You don't need to "know" grammar to find them. Your ear will tell you.

If your ear does find a sick sentence, however, you will be better off knowing some grammatical terms and concepts so that you can diagnose and correct errors or recognize and improve weaknesses. That is what the rest of this book is about.

As you begin to read this discussion of grammar, you will hit terms that may initially seem a bit confusing. Grammar, unfortunately, is a circular subject: you can't understand A until you know X, but you can't know X without understanding A through W. So if at first the terms seem a shade incomprehensible, don't despair. Just try to grasp the general

concepts and keep going. Things will clear up as the terms repeat and reinforce one another.

It's time now for some preliminary definitions.

The word **grammar,** as we shall be using it, refers to a
study of the forms, structures, and functions of a language. We
met this definition earlier, in Chapter 3. Now we can examine
its terms more closely.

First, **form.** We can look upon words as the fundamental
units of written grammar. Words have specific spellings. The
arrangement of letters in a word gives it a shape or form. Some
words can change their forms for certain purposes: a noun may
add an -*s* when it is plural, or a verb may add -*ed* in the past
tense. The term *form* will be used to refer both to a word and
to the special changes that can be made in it to show different
grammatical characteristics. Thus, we could say that *babies* is
the plural form of *baby.* Obviously, form is quite basic—so basic
that you probably began to learn spelling in first grade and
studied rules like "change -*y* to -*i* and add -*es*" to turn *baby*
into *babies* long before junior high school. Knowing when to
use what form is a prerequisite for all writing.

Words (or forms) are sometimes classified into categories
known as **parts of speech.** Some grammatical systems list eight
parts of speech, some nine, some several dozen. We can make
do with seven: nouns, pronouns, verbs, adjectives, adverbs,
prepositions, and conjunctions. Very roughly, nouns and pronouns represent things that we wish to talk about, verbs represent actions or states of some sort, adjectives describe things,
adverbs describe actions, and both prepositions and conjunctions show connecting relationships between words or word
groups. These definitions are neither complete nor totally
accurate, but they will suffice to get us started.

Although forms are fundamental, they are in themselves
lifeless and uncommunicative. If you imagine a mammoth
listing of dictionary entries minus their definitions, you'd have
a catalogue of all the forms of English. But the forms could
transmit no message unless they were put together with proper

structure and function. These last two terms add utility and fascination to grammar, because by playing games with forms, we introduce creativity into language.

A grammatical **structure** is a sequence of related forms. English has but two basic kinds of structures—phrases and clauses. Each kind, however, has several varieties, as we shall see later. Just as you put certain forms of wood and nails together to build the structure of a table (or a coat rack), so too you put certain forms of words together to build the structure of a prepositional phrase (or a dependent clause). When you join word forms together into structures, you must follow the rules of **syntax**, the permissible ways to arrange forms to create specific structures. Syntactical rules are somewhat akin to blueprints: one blueprint for tables or prepositional phrases, another blueprint for coat racks or dependent clauses.

In carpentry, the **function** that you want accomplished influences the structure that you build. If you want a surface to eat upon, you build a table rather than a coat rack. So in one sense, the desired function determines the choice of structure. But a given structure might serve several functions: you can eat at a table, but you can also write at it, or play cards on it, or even stand on it. In another sense, then, the structure of an object determines its possible functions, the uses to which it can be put. The two concepts are somewhat chicken-and-eggish.

Structure and function are similarly intertwined in grammar. There is little point in building a grammatical structure unless you have some function you wish it to perform, but a given structure might perform several functions, and a given function might be filled by many different structures. Take a prepositional phrase. Like a table, this particular structure can perform several functions: it can act (rarely) as the subject of a clause and (most commonly) as a modifier for a noun or a verb. Because of its structure, a prepositional phrase can't do anything else. But many other structures can perform one of these functions, as subjects or as modifiers. These are two of the most important functions in grammar, so we have a plentiful choice of structures to perform them.

Before looking at other functions, we need to make one point: forms have functions, just as structures have functions. Let's consider a sentence containing a prepositional phrase: *The ball rolled down the hill*. The prepositional phrase *down the hill* modifies (or describes) the verb *rolled:* that is the function of the total phrase. But within the phrase, each word form has its own function: *hill* functions as the object of the preposition *down, the* functions as a modifier of *hill*, and *down* functions dually to introduce the phrase and to relate *hill* to *rolled*. So forms have definite functions within structures, and smaller structures have definite functions within larger structures. Form, structure, function: the three braided strands of grammar.

Grammatical functions are relatively few. Let's look briefly at three important ones. A form or a structure can function as the **subject** of a sentence. The subject indicates what you are talking about: *Flowers grow. Very few television shows are worth watching*. Next, a form or a structure can function as the **predicate** of a sentence. The predicate indicates what you say about the subject: *Flowers grow. Very few television shows are worth watching*. You obviously couldn't say much without words that function as subject and as predicate. These functions are essential.

The one other fundamental function that we need to consider at this point is **modification**. Modifiers are forms or structures that identify, change, limit, explain, or otherwise give descriptive information about nouns and verbs. Without modifiers, all our sentences would be as stark as *Flowers grow*. With modifiers, a sentence can become just as precise and colorful as we wish: *Bowing gracefully on their stalks, brilliant red flowers grow in lush profusion along the river banks*. Here, the first seven words modify *flowers*, and the last seven modify *grow*. With these fourteen added words, the sentence comes to life. Modification, too, is clearly essential.

To review the concepts we've met so far, we shall examine the **grammar** of a simple sentence:

> *The red book with the gold lettering was lying on the table.*

The first thing we might notice is the **form** of the words. Each of them is spelled correctly. We could also observe that *was* is a past tense form of *to be* and that *lying* is a special form of *to lie.* We could classify each of these words as a **part of speech**, calling *book* and *table* nouns, for instance, or *was lying* a verb form, or *red* and *gold* adjectives.

Next, we might isolate the various **structures** in this sentence. Small structures nest inside larger structures that nest inside still larger structures. Eventually we reach the largest structure, the entire sentence itself. If someone were to ask you to split the sentence into small sequences of words that seem to "go together," you certainly wouldn't split it, say, like this:

> *The red / book with the gold / lettering was / lying on the / table.*

You'd probably end up with the following chunks:

> *The red book / with the gold lettering / was lying / on the table.*

And if you then looked for larger structures, you'd most likely group the smaller chunks this way:

> *The red book with the gold lettering / was lying on the table.*

Finally, as we said, the entire sentence is the largest structure, encompassing all the smaller structures.

Each of the chunks has its special structural name. *With the gold lettering* and *on the table* are called prepositional phrases, *the red book* is a noun phrase, and *was lying* is a verb phrase. Also, each of these chunks has its special **function**: *with the gold lettering,* for example, **modifies** *the red book; on the table* **modifies** *was lying. The red book with the gold lettering* functions as the **subject** of the sentence, and *was lying on the table* functions as its **predicate**.

Finally, it is the rules of **syntax** that tell us how to put words and chunks together, so that we write *the red book* and not *red the book* or *was lying on the table* and not *on the table lying was.*

Already we can make a fairly complete grammatical analysis of this particular sentence. That is, we can say things about the sentence and how it works, using the special jargon of grammarians. In the next chapter we shall look at some of the more troublesome forms and learn a few more technical terms, so that we can talk with even greater precision about the sentences we write.

5

A Minimum
of Definitions

Once upon a time (and perhaps even today), grammar study was mostly devoted to labeling the words in a sentence. If you could identify all the nouns and verbs and prepositions and adverbs, you passed the course. But you seldom learned what to do with these pieces after you named them. It was like being able to name spark plugs and piston rods and gaskets and head bolts but never learning how to put an engine together, let alone understanding how it works.

In this book you will learn a great deal about how to build sentences and how to make their parts fit together in different ways to achieve different effects. Understanding the structure and the function of grammatical units lets you create your own well-crafted prose. First, though, it is still necessary to "name the parts" so that we can share a common vocabulary with which to talk about grammar.

Of the seven parts of speech that you need to recognize, nouns are the most familiar. A noun, you probably recall, is "the name of a person, place, or thing." The old definition has its faults, but it is a safe guide. Most people can label nouns accurately enough. Just as a reminder, though, every noun in this paragraph has been underlined. Any questions?

The **pronoun** category contains a raft of little words—*you, me, them, she, it, his, who, none, himself, someone,* just as a small sample. The various forms of pronouns can get very detailed and quite confusing. Chapter 31, "Agreement," looks at some of the stickier points of pronouns, but if you really want to understand these pesky forms, you should check a comprehensive survey of grammar. For our immediate purposes, you need to know only two things about pronouns. First, pronouns are often used to replace nouns that otherwise would have to be repeated. Thus, instead of saying *Mary kissed John because Mary liked John,* we say *Mary kissed John because she liked him.* In such situations, pronouns work just like nouns, building the same kinds of structures and performing the same kinds of functions. So whatever is said hereafter about nouns would be equally true of any pronouns that might replace them. Second, a pronoun must always agree with the noun it represents. If the noun is singular, the pronoun must be singular; if the noun is masculine, the pronoun must be masculine. Because these and other considerations can be a bit troublesome, we shall explore them at some length in Chapter 31. Meanwhile, we can relegate the finer points of pronouns to more technical grammars.

Verbs are every bit as complex as pronouns. They also, however, happen to be the most important words in grammar, so we can't brush them aside as casually as we did pronouns. Verbs are important because they are the one essential element in a grammatical English sentence. The single word *Listen!* can suffice as a grammatical sentence, and any longer collection of words must have at least one verb if it is to be a sentence. But just any verb form won't work, so here is where complications arise, complications that must be understood to understand grammar.

A verb is the only kind of English word that changes its form to reflect changes in time. The difference between *He drives the car* and *He drove the car* is merely a change in the form of the verb, from *drives* to *drove;* but this small change indicates significant differences in the times of the two actions.

The grammatical term for the time of an action is **tense,** so we can say that the form of the verb indicates the tense of its sentence. Now comes the important point to remember: Every grammatical sentence must contain a verb form that indicates tense.

There is a catch, of course. Not every verb form shows tense without some kind of help. Each verb has five forms (sometimes called "principle parts"), and only two of these forms can, by themselves, mark the tense of a sentence. Take the verb *drive,* for example. *He drives the car* shows the present tense, and the verb form makes a good sentence. *He drove the car* shows the past tense, and again the sentence is grammatical. But there are two more forms called **participles.** For *drive,* the present participle is *driving;* the past participle is *driven.* Do not let the words "present" and "past" in these terms confuse you: participles when used alone do <u>not</u> show the tense of a sentence. Thus, neither *He driving the car* nor *He driven the car* qualifies as a good English sentence. The fifth and final form is the **infinitive,** *to drive.* It, too, lacks an ability to show tense, so we can't have this as a sentence: *He to drive the car.*

The two participial forms (*driving* and *driven*) and the infinitive form (*to drive*) are called **verbals** because they are closely related to the kinds of verbs that can be used to make a sentence. Both verbals and verbs can be followed by objects (in these examples, *the car*), and both can be modified by adverbs (*He drove the car recklessly* and *driving the car recklessly*). But there is an essential distinction between true verbs and verbals. Only true verbs—those usable as the main verb of a sentence— show tense. They are specifically limited by time; or, as we grammarians say, they are **finite.** A finite verb form, then, is a verb form that indicates the tense of its sentence, so that we can now rephrase the point emphasized above: **Every grammatical sentence must contain a finite verb form.**

Because verbals are not finite, they cannot function as main verbs of sentences. As we shall see later, infinitives can function like adverbs; infinitives and present participles can serve many of the same functions as nouns; infinitives and both present and past participles can function like adjectives. All three verbals also share another important duty: they can help to build finite verb phrases.

English actually has only two simple tenses, the present tense (*He drives the car*) and the past tense (*He drove the car*). Obviously, though, we are not limited to these two constricting ideas of time. English is peculiarly rich in its array of nuances to show not only times but also conditions, possibilities, probabilities, hopes, continuities, and completions of actions in the present, in the distant or recent past, or in the future. We show all these shades of meaning through **finite verb phrases**, aggregations of one or more verbals preceded by appropriate **auxiliaries**. These auxiliaries are "helping verbs," words like *is, were, have, did, will, should, must, can,* and half a dozen others. The final verbal in a verb phrase gives the "verb-ish" meaning to the phrase; the auxiliary shows its tense. With the tense-marked auxiliary, the whole verb phrase becomes finite, usable as a main verb for a sentence.

The careful combination of auxiliaries and verbals permits us to gain an ultimate of precision in describing an action. For example, *He **had been** able to work* shows through its finite verb phrase a factual situation in the distant past, with the implication that a more recent past situation is also involved in the picture. Now consider how different auxiliaries influence the case:

> *He **should have been** able to work.*
> *He **might have been** able to work.*
> *He **would have been** able to work.*
> *He **may have been** able to work.*
> *He **could have been** able to work.*

Each of those sentences creates its own specific suggestion of actuality, implausibility, doubt, disappointment, or irritation. The modulations are yours to control.

If you remember that verbals (that is, participles and infinitives) cannot act alone as main verbs, and if you know how to manipulate verbs and verb phrases, you are well on your way to gaining that subtle control over sentences made possible by the beautiful flexibility of the English verb system. But despite its functional flexibility, the system is structured along rigid and rather complex rules. For the moment, just try to grasp the main outline of grammatical concepts being drawn here. To avoid interrupting this survey with details, essential though they are, we shall postpone until Chapter 30 a full breakdown of verbs and verb phrases. You will, however, be meeting finite verb forms, participles, and infinitives throughout the remainder of the book, so be warned.

There should be little need to define **adjectives**; they are words that modify nouns, like *yellow roses, his car,* and *hard work.* Adverbs are slightly more complicated. Basically, an **adverb** is a word that modifies a verb. Adverbs modify verbs three ways: by time, place, and manner. An *adverb of time* tells <u>when</u> an action occurs: *The dog barked **yesterday**.* An *adverb of place* tells <u>where</u> it occurs: *The dog barked **outside**.* And an *adverb of manner* tells <u>how</u> it occurs: *The dog barked **frantically**.* Adverbs can also modify complete sentences: ***Finally**, the war ended.* Some grammars assert that adverbs modify adjectives and other adverbs—which is true enough if you wish to set up a grammatical system that labels every word in English. It has been said that "adverb" is a grab-bag category: if you can't find anything else to call a word, call it an adverb. As a result, all sorts of strange bits and pieces of English get tossed into the adverb bag. Our purpose, however, is not to apply labels but to understand form, structure, and function. It suffices, in this book, to limit ourselves to a partial but useful truth: adverbs are words that modify verbs and sentences.

One more group of words needs to be looked at. These words are prepositions, conjunctions, and a category we haven't yet mentioned, transitional words. They are grouped here because they all serve the same general function: to connect or relate one set of words to another set. You may recall the three fundamental functions of grammatical units discussed earlier: to act as a **subject**, as a **predicate**, and as a **modifier**. We now meet the fourth and last fundamental function: to act as a **connector**. Every form or structure of English serves in one of these four major functions.

Let us begin with prepositions. A **preposition** is a word or group of words that relates one noun to another noun or to a verb. Take *the tree in the yard*, for example: the preposition *in* shows the relationship between *yard* and *tree*. Or consider *ran around the corner*, in which *around* relates *corner* to *ran*. The relationship may show a rather general association of the two words (*of, with, for*, etc.), a time sequence (*before, during, after*, etc.), or a position in space (*in, over, behind, in front of, on top of, under, near*, etc.).

The noun that accompanies the preposition is called the **object of the preposition**, and a preposition must always have an object. It is, in fact, the necessity of having an object that distinguishes prepositions from similar-appearing words; for, without the object, a preposition could not be a connector. Consider *He looked down the cliff. Down* is a preposition connecting its object, *cliff*, to the verb *looked*. But then consider *He looked down*. The same word, *down*, but no object. So here *down* cannot be a preposition. Instead it is—you guessed it—an adverb. The object normally follows immediately after its preposition: *over the hill; beyond the foreseeable future*. In some situations, however, the object may appear earlier in the sentence, as in an informal question (*Which painting did the judges give the prize to?*) or in a poetic inversion (*He roamed the wide world over*).

To move now from prepositions to **conjunctions**. As their name suggests, conjunctions join or connect words or groups of words. The most obvious conjunction is probably the common little word *and: sticks and stones; jumping the fence and swimming the stream*. Conjunctions come in three varieties: coordinating, correlative, and subordinating. **Subordinating con-**

junctions are words like *because, if, although,* and *when.* They serve but one purpose: to introduce dependent clauses, connecting them to independent clauses. We shall look at them later when we discuss clauses. That leaves the two **co-** varieties to examine now.

English has only seven **coordinating conjunctions:** *and, but, or, nor, for, so,* and *yet.* You might as well memorize them, for they have a few special characteristics that influence how you use them. **Correlative conjunctions** come in pairs, and English has but three of these pairs: *either . . . or, neither . . . nor,* and *not only . . . but (also).* (The *also* is placed within parentheses here because it is optional; you usually use *but also* after *not only,* although you may at times choose to omit *also* if it sounds unnecessary.) Learn these, too, and then you will know, by the process of elimination, that all other conjunctions are subordinating.

The seven coordinating conjunctions and the three pairs of correlative conjunctions are the only words that can connect two independent clauses—the conjunctive function of particular concern to us in this book. Other correlative pairs exist (such as *whether . . . or, as . . . as, not . . . but,* or *both . . . and*), but they can't join independent clauses. Instead, they connect smaller elements, like nouns, perhaps, or adjectives, or even dependent clauses.

The one most important thing you should know about both coordinating and correlative conjunctions is that they must join two or more equal grammatical units. English has very few absolute rules. You have already met one of them: **Every grammatical sentence must contain a finite verb form.** Now you are meeting a second rule: **Coordinating and correlative conjunctions must join equal grammatical units.**

Let's see what this means. A grammatical unit might be a noun, an adjective, a verb, a participle, or one of the two larger units, phrases and clauses. A noun would be equal to a noun, but not to a verb phrase, for example. Hence, a coordinating conjunction like *and* can make the following junctions: noun + noun, verb + verb, adjective + adjective, prepositional phrase + prepositional phrase, and so forth. As long as the units are equal, they can be joined by a coordinating conjunction. That's why we can say *I need **food and clothes***, with *and* joining two nouns, but not *I need **to eat and clothes***, with *and* joining an infinitive and a noun. In a simple example like this, the error is obvious. In more complex sentences, you need to keep an eye on your conjunctions to make sure that coordinating or correlative conjunctions actually join grammatically equal units.

Finally, there are the somewhat tricky items that we shall call **transitional words** or **sentence connectors**. These are words or groups of words that show a logical relation between two sentences. Examples include *moreover, thus, therefore, still, however,* and *on the other hand.* They are tricky because some people confuse them with the conjunctions that we have just looked at. But note that transitional words indicate logical relations between sentences, not grammatical connections within a sentence. Grammatically, these words are the kind of adverbs that modify whole sentences, the kind we met in the earlier example, ***Finally,** the war ended.* Logically, they connect the ideas of two separate sentences: *Congress passed a tax-cut bill.* ***However,** the president vetoed it.* Here, the logical relation is a reversal or denial in the second sentence of the idea in the first sentence. We will look more closely at logical relations in Chapter 26. All you should remember at the moment is that transitional words connect the <u>ideas</u> of sentences. They are <u>not</u> grammatical conjunctions.

To forestall possible objections here, it should be pointed out that a transitional word can appear in the middle of a sentence, as in *Congress passed a tax-cut bill; however, the president vetoed it.* In this situation, the transitional word shows the logical relation between two independent clauses (discussed in the next chapter). It is still not a conjunction; the clauses are joined by the semicolon.

6

Word Chunks:
Sentences and Clauses

It's time now to move from form to structure, that is, from individual word classifications to chunks of words fitting together into recognizable units. These structural units have names: sentences, clauses, and phrases. The first we shall consider is also the largest—the sentence.

We have been using the term *sentence* rather freely so far, on the safe assumption that everyone is familiar with the word. But from now on, we must differentiate between two distinct meanings of *sentence*.

A **typographical sentence** is any word or collection of words beginning with a capital letter and ending with a period, a question mark, an exclamation point, or even a dash or three dots. These are the written clues to where a typographical sentence starts and stops. Thus, all of the following examples could be effective typographical sentences.

The time is ripe.
Why me again?
Ouch!
They might have won, if only . . .

A **grammatical sentence** is also any word or collection of words beginning with a capital and closing with a mark of terminal punctuation. But the words must combine a subject (stated or implied) with a predicate, and the predicate must contain a finite verb form. According to this definition, of the typographical sentences given above only *The time is ripe* is grammatical. In other words, every grammatical sentence is typographical, but not every typographical sentence is grammatical. Grammatical sentences range from single words like *Stop!* (with *you* as the implied subject), to short cryptic statements like *She did so,* to most of the sentences that you see in print.

Notice that the term *sentence* has nothing to do with a group of words that conveys a complete idea, as many books define it. There is certainly no "complete idea" in *She did so.* We know neither who she is nor what she did. But the sentence is grammatical. It has a subject, *she,* and a predicate, *did so.* That's all it needs to be a grammatical sentence.

Because many good, effective sentences are not grammatically complete, it is sometimes necessary to distinguish typographical sentences from grammatical sentences. Usually we shall merely use the term *sentence* to refer to words between a capital and a period. Where the distinction is pertinent, however, the more specific terms will be used.

To review briefly, a grammatical sentence begins with a capital, ends with a mark of terminal punctuation, and needs a subject–predicate combination. The subject is the person or thing you talk about; the predicate is what you say about the subject: *The Senate* (subject) *approved the treaty* (predicate). The subject is missing in sentences that give a command: *Come here.* We say in cases like this that the subject is "*you,* understood." The predicate, however, can never be missing. Remember, too, that the essential part of every predicate is a finite verb form, one that is marked for tense. For the moment, that is enough on sentences.

There are but two large classes of structural units in

English grammar: clauses and phrases. A **clause** is a set of related words having a subject–predicate combination. A **phrase** is a set of related words lacking a subject–predicate combination. If it occurs to you that a sentence must also be a clause, you are quite right. A sentence is one kind of clause, an independent clause. The other kind is a dependent clause, which comes in three varieties. There are six varieties of phrases. We have met two so far—the verb phrase like *had driven,* which lacks a subject, and the prepositional phrase like *across the road,* consisting of a preposition and its object, but obviously devoid of either subject or predicate. We shall meet the other four varieties in the next chapter.

The best place to start is with the larger unit, the clause, and more specifically with the **independent clause.** Everything stated two paragraphs back about the grammatical sentence could also be true of the independent clause, for an independent clause is a clause that can stand alone as a grammatical sentence. Conversely, every grammatical sentence has at least one independent clause, although it may have more than one, plus attached dependent clauses. This statement is so fundamental that it needs to be repeated, as one of the "musts" of written grammar: **A grammatical sentence must have at least one independent clause.** Here are some examples of independent clauses written as typographical sentences:

Inflation erodes the dollar.
His poems are immortal.
Natural resources should be conserved.

A **dependent clause** is a clause that starts with a subordinating conjunction or a relative pronoun. Because of these introductory elements, dependent clauses cannot stand alone as grammatical sentences. They must always be attached somehow to an independent clause, where they function like adverbs, adjectives, or nouns. Independent clauses can easily be transformed into dependent clauses, as we see here:

> *because inflation erodes the dollar*
> *whose poems are immortal*
> *that natural resources should be conserved*

These three examples represent the three varieties of dependent clauses—the adverbial clause, the relative or adjectival clause, and the noun clause. Each variety has its special function. Let's begin with adverbial clauses.

An **adverbial clause** is a dependent clause headed by a **subordinating conjunction,** a word like *because, if, when, although, since, whether, before,* and *whereas,* or a word group like *even though, as long as,* and *despite the fact that.* Subordinating conjunctions join only clauses, and only clauses of unequal grammatical rank. That is, the dependent clause (the one headed by the subordinating conjunction) must be joined to a higher-ranked independent clause. We might join the adverbial clause *because inflation erodes the dollar* to an independent clause, *we must curb rising prices,* to build this sentence:

> *We must curb rising prices **because inflation erodes the dollar**.*

As the name *adverbial clause* suggests, this kind of dependent clause functions just like an adverb, modifying either the verb of the independent clause or the entire independent clause. Compare these two sentences:

> *We must curb rising prices **immediately**.* (adverb)
> *We must curb rising prices **as soon as we can**.* (adverbial clause)

In each sentence, the boldfaced portion modifies the verb *must curb.* The single word *immediately* is an adverb; the dependent clause *as soon as we can* acts like an adverb—it is an **adverbial**. We will meet the term *adverbial* again whenever we find groups of words functioning like single adverbs. The adverbial clause, then, is just an overgrown adverb, complete with subject and predicate.

A word of explanation may be in order here. Some subordinating conjunctions look exactly like prepositions. They have the same form but not the same function. For example, *before, after, since,* and *while* might be either subordinating conjunctions or prepositions, depending on how they are used. A subordinating conjunction always connects a dependent clause to an independent clause: *She left after she ate breakfast.* A preposition relates its object—a noun or a noun substitute—to some word in a clause: *She left after eating breakfast* (a participial phrase as the object of *after;* you'll hear more of participial phrases shortly) or *She left after breakfast* (a noun as the object). Both prepositional phrases modify the verb *left.* Remember, then, that a subordinating conjunction is followed by the subject–predicate combination of its dependent clause; a preposition is followed by a noun or anything that acts like a noun.

The second variety of dependent clauses is the **relative clause**, also called an **adjectival clause** because it functions like an adjective. Similar to the term *adverbial,* an **adjectival** is a word (other than an adjective) or a group of words that modifies a noun, just as a single adjective does. An adjectival clause is headed by a relative pronoun—*who* (*whom, whose*), *which,* or *that.* The relative pronoun replaces a noun or personal pronoun (like *she, they, it*) in its clause, thereby both creating an adjectival clause and relating that clause to some noun in an independent clause. This sounds confusing. To look at it one step at a time, let us return to our sample sentence:

His poems are immortal.

First, replace the possessive personal pronoun *his* with the possessive relative pronoun *whose:*

> *whose poems are immortal*

Now we have an adjectival clause that can be used to modify the noun *John Keats* in this independent clause:

> *John Keats died relatively unknown.*

Here is what we would end up with:

> *John Keats, **whose poems are immortal,** died relatively unknown.*

The relative clause, as we can see, is nothing but a bulky noun modifier, an adjectival.

The third and last variety of dependent clause is the **noun clause.** A noun clause is headed by *that* or words like *what, where, whoever,* and a few others. Although in structure it somewhat resembles an adverbial clause, you can recognize a noun clause by its function. A noun clause acts just like a noun, functioning usually as the subject of a larger clause or as the object of a verb. Here are two examples:

> **That natural resources should be conserved** *is indisputable.* (noun clause functioning as subject of sentence)
> *Most people understand* **that natural resources should be conserved.** (noun clause functioning as object of verb *understand*)

Noun clauses are rather common constructions, especially after what might be called "verbs of cognition"—*know, realize, believe, understand, recognize, remember, feel,* and others. A few more examples of noun clauses may be useful.

*She knows **what she wants**.* (object of verb *knows*)

***Whoever painted this picture** has true talent.* (subject)

*He remembered **how the system worked**.* (object of verb *remembered*)

*Give help to **whoever needs it**.* (object of preposition *to*)

We have looked now at the independent clause and at the three kinds of dependent clauses: the adverbial, the adjectival, and the noun clause. One final point should be mentioned. Every kind of clause follows the same basic **word order**. The term *word order* refers to the sequential order or position of grammatical units in a structure. Clauses normally follow one fundamental pattern of word order:

CLAUSE → SUBJECT + PREDICATE

And the predicate normally shows a standard word order:

PREDICATE → FINITE VERB FORM (+ optional elements)

Although the word order of a clause may be juggled somewhat for specific reasons, as we shall see later, this basic pattern is so important that it can be included as one of the few "musts" of grammar: **The normal word order of a clause is SUBJECT plus PREDICATE.**

On this firm note, we can leave clauses and turn to phrases.

7

Word Chunks: Phrases

Phrases are next on the agenda. A **phrase** is a set of related words that has no subject–predicate combination. There's no way phrases can act as grammatical sentences. Instead, they always serve some kind of function within a clause. Five kinds of phrases are sufficiently common to warrant their own names: noun phrases, verb phrases, prepositional phrases, participial phrases, and infinitive phrases. A sixth variety has a special name, the absolute. We shall look at each of these in turn.

A **noun phrase** is merely a noun with all its attached modifiers: *the biggest, brightest star in the galaxy; all the highly polished, chrome-trimmed automobiles.* Each noun phrase has one main word, the **head noun**, that all the other words in the phrase modify. The words *star* and *automobiles* are the head nouns of their respective phrases. Noun phrases can be used anywhere simple nouns are used: as subjects, as objects of verbs or prepositions, or in other noun functions. Thus,

> *The telescope focused on the biggest, brightest star in the galaxy.* (object of preposition *on*)
> *All the highly polished, chrome-trimmed automobiles were valuable antiques.* (subject)

We have already discussed verb phrases—combinations of verbals and tense-marked auxiliary verbs such as *had been running* or *will have finished*. Verb phrases act like any other finite verb form, to provide the nucleus of a clause predicate.

Prepositional phrases should also be familiar to you by now. They combine a preposition with its object, the object being a noun or any other element that functions like a noun—a noun phrase, perhaps, or a noun clause. Infrequently, a prepositional phrase functions like a noun, as when it acts as the subject of a sentence:

> *After seven is the best time to call.*

Usually, though, a prepositional phrase acts as an adjectival (to modify a noun) or as an adverbial (to modify a verb or a whole sentence):

> *The headlines **in the morning paper** were reassuring.*
> (an adjectival, modifying the noun *headlines*)
> *The knee bone is connected **to the thigh bone**.* (an adverbial, modifying the verb *is connected*)
> ***In the long run**, most houses appreciate in value.* (an adverbial, modifying the entire sentence)

A **participial phrase** consists of a participle plus related words, like an object or modifiers. As you recall, participles are verb forms that come in two varieties: present participles, such as *rotating* and *prosecuting,* and past participles, such as *broken* and *satisfied.* We could use these examples to make participial phrases:

> *rotating the disc slowly on its spindle*
> *prosecuting the case*
> *broken by careless treatment*
> *clearly satisfied with the outcome*

Phrases built with present participles serve two functions: as noun replacements (when they are also called *gerunds*) and as adjectivals. Here is a participial phrase functioning like a noun, as the subject of its sentence:

> *Rotating the disc slowly on its spindle sets the machine into operation.*

And here the participial phrase is an adjectival, modifying the noun *attorney:*

> *The attorney **prosecuting the case** lacked experience.*

Phrases built with past participles can only function as adjectivals:

> *This guarantee does not cover equipment **broken by careless treatment.*** (modifies the noun *equipment*)
> ***Clearly satisfied with the outcome**, the doctor left the operating room.* (modifies the noun *doctor*)

Like a participial phrase, an **infinitive phrase** consists of a verbal plus associated words—an object, an adverb, or perhaps both. Here are three examples of infinitive phrases:

> *to bowl a perfect game*
> *to cherish for life*
> *to perfect their strokes*

Infinitive phrases serve three main functions. They can act as nouns, as adjectivals, and as adverbials. In this sentence, the infinitive phrase serves as a noun, as the subject of its sentence:

> *To bowl a perfect game takes as much luck as skill.*

In this one, the infinitive phrase acts as an adjectival, modifying the noun *memories:*

> *The trip provided her with memories **to cherish for life**.*

And here the infinitive phrase functions as an adverbial, modifying the verb *practice:*

> *Star tennis players practice daily **to perfect their strokes**.*

Infinitive phrases also appear in many idiomatic expressions: *to coin a phrase, to put it mildly, to speak bluntly, to tell the truth,* and others. Such expressions are usually tacked onto sentences as modifiers of the entire attached statement. As such, they could be called adverbials. However, since this use of infinitive phrases seldom raises any problems in writing, there is no need to worry about the function.

The last kind of phrase we shall look at is the **absolute**, a rather unusual kind of construction that requires some explanation. An absolute is a noun–participle combination or a noun–adjective combination. It functions as a more or less separate unit, with no specific grammatical relation to the clause it accompanies. Instead, the <u>idea</u> of the absolute merely has a general connection to the <u>idea</u> of its attached clause. Here is an absolute formed with a participle:

> *Congress having adjourned, the representatives went home to their districts.*

Here the absolute is formed with an adjective:

> *His voice firm, the accused pled "not guilty."*

An absolute is a handy device for packing additional ideas neatly and tersely within the confines of a sentence. Similarly neat and terse is the appositive, a unit defined by its function rather than its structure. We can examine it next.

An **appositive** is not a specific kind of clause or phrase; it is simply any word or group of words that renames, defines, describes, or identifies a noun mentioned in the same sentence as the appositive. But the appositive is related to its noun companion only by juxtaposition and not by any grammatical link. Usually the appositive directly follows the noun or noun phrase to which it relates:

> *Watson and Crick uncovered the secret of heredity, **the double helix**.*

Here, the appositive is *the double helix*; it identifies *the secret of heredity*. Occasionally, the appositive precedes its related noun:

> ***Agriculture, industry, security, health***—*these areas are but a few of the government's concerns.*

In this sentence, the four-noun appositive gives specific names to *these areas*.

Adjectives can also function like appositives:

> *The federal budget, **bulky, detailed, and complex**, defies anyone's comprehension.*

Bulky, detailed, and complex serve to describe and further identify *the federal budget*. And noun clauses may function as appositives, especially when they define a noun like *fact*:

> *The fact **that he was late** annoyed her.*
> *His weak excuse, **that he had to work overtime**, failed to convince her.*

This is one more proof that a noun clause functions just like a noun.

You have seen several such groups of words that act like nouns. Since you already know the terms *adjectival* and *adverbial*, you should know as well the related term *nominal*. A **nominal** is, not surprisingly, a word (other than a noun), phrase, or clause that functions like a noun. The following sentence has two nominals:

> *To prepare for an oral examination requires hours of studying.*

The first nominal, *to prepare for an oral examination,* is an infinitive phrase functioning as the subject of the sentence; the second nominal, *studying,* is a present participle functioning as the object of a preposition. Since both functions are normally filled by nouns, the infinitive phrase and the participle are nominals in this particular sentence.

You may now take a deep breath. You've been introduced to a slew of terms, but they cover almost all the words you need if you want to talk about grammar. Those terms you didn't already know will become familiar to you as they reappear in the following chapters. Before we continue, though, a quick recap may be helpful.

8

A Reprise

You've just read through a rather lengthy roll of preliminary facts—lots of characters but not much plot. You should be ready now to move on to the interesting part of grammar: finding out how these forms, structures, and functions are combined to produce good writing. First, however, a fast review.

Several statements in the preceding chapters were in boldface. These statements represent four of the absolutely essential rules of English grammar. There are only seven such "musts" to remember. All the other rules or principles stem from those seven. Here are the first four again, regrouped for easy reference.

1. *A grammatical sentence must have at least one independent clause.*
2. *The normal word order of a clause is*
   SUBJECT + PREDICATE
   $\longrightarrow$ *VERB (+ optional elements).*
3. *The main verb of a clause must be finite in form.*
4. *Coordinating and correlative conjunctions must join equal grammatical units.*

The remaining three rules deal with agreement between subjects and their verbs and between pronouns and their referents. These rules can be postponed until Chapter 31, where we shall look at some of the problems of agreement.

Taken together, the seven essential rules are all you really need to understand in order to write correctly. No doubt the first four seem quite familiar to you. In fact, you've probably been following them in your writing, consciously or unconsciously. It is actually your <u>un</u>conscious knowledge of grammar that guides most of your language use. By now, though, you should be ready to put some conscious knowledge to work. Turn the page.

III

The Independent Clause

9

Clauses
and Other Fragments

We shall begin our examination of grammatical structures with the independent clause, and with a reminder that the independent clause consists of a subject and a predicate, in that order. The subject is usually the first unit in the clause. (For the moment, we are looking only at declarative statements and ignoring questions and stylistic inversions, where the subject may be displaced from its initial position.) At times you will find some introductory element preceding the subject—in this sentence, the prepositional phrase *at times;* in other sentences, perhaps an adverb, a coordinating conjunction, a participial phrase, or a dependent clause. But if these introductory elements are shaved off, what remains within the independent clause itself is the subject–predicate combination—only.

Contrast this with what we find in a dependent clause. Again, it will have a subject and a predicate; otherwise, it would not qualify as a clause. But the first word of any dependent clause will be either a subordinating conjunction or a relative pronoun. And neither of these words can be "shaved off" without changing the dependent nature of the clause. They form an essential part of the dependent clause. (We shall later note some apparent exceptions to this statement and, still later, the reason why those exceptions do not really contradict the statement after all. Remember, then, that a subordinating conjunction or a relative pronoun is an essential part of its dependent clause.)

Here lies the distinction between an independent and a dependent clause, and here too lies one source of sentence fragments. An independent clause can be punctuated as a grammatical sentence, but a dependent clause cannot. Suppose someone writes *Whereas additional funding will not be forthcoming.* (The asterisk labels chunks of words that do not form a grammatical sentence.) The initial capital and the final period make these words a typographical sentence. But the subordinating conjunction *whereas* turns the words into a dependent clause—a fragment, a piece of a sentence masquerading as a complete sentence.

Both the independent and the dependent clauses need a predicate, and the predicate must have a finite verb form. A finite verb form, you recall, is limited or defined by tense. Either the form of a single verb or the form of an auxiliary in a verb phrase must somehow be marked to indicate the time of the verb's action. A participial form alone, like *running* or *eaten,* can't do it. Neither can an infinitive like *to speak:* the very word *infinitive* tells you the form is non-finite, tenseless. When a typographical sentence has a non-finite verb form, we have a second source of sentence fragments. Someone may write *The reason being the high cost of energy.* Again, the capital and the period mark this as a typographical sentence. But *being* is a participle; it is not finite. So what we have here punctuated as a sentence is really just a noun–participle combination—an absolute, a sentence fragment.

As long as we are discussing fragments, let's look at the third obvious kind of fragment, the typographical sentence that lacks both a subject and a finite verb. Perhaps the sentence is merely a string of adjectives: *Thick, juicy, and rare in the middle.* This might be a quite adequate answer to the question *How do you like your steak?* But it's still a fragment.

Sentence fragments are *per se* neither good nor bad. It all depends on how you use them, and when, and where. Serious formal writing hardly ever contains fragments. The somewhat less formal kind of good writing that you find, say, in the *Atlantic Monthly* or *Esquire* might have rather frequent fragments. Given the right subject, audience, and tone, a fragment can at times prove more effective than a complete grammatical sentence. But the point is, you should recognize a fragment when you write it. If you deliberately wish to use a fragment, and if your ear and your instinct tell you it is effective, and if it does not seem out of place in the kind of writing you are doing, then fair enough—use it. It is the fragment written <u>non</u>-deliberately, through carelessness or ignorance, that can cause trouble.

A fragment might cause trouble, not because it "violates a rule," but because it undermines your readers' expectations. Readers expect a typographical sentence to be a grammatical sentence. If instead it is a fragment—and not an obviously deliberate, effective fragment—your readers may be puzzled. They'll think they've missed something, back up and read the sentence again, and realize that the sentence is indeed incomplete. Then they are slowed down and annoyed because they've lost their chain of thought—and you may have lost some readers.

To recap, an independent clause must not begin with a subordinating conjunction or a relative pronoun. And it must contain a subject and a predicate, with a finite verb form in the predicate. In the next chapter we are going to split the subject from the predicate so that we can concentrate on what the subject is and what we can do with it.

10

Clause Subjects

Within a clause (independent or dependent), you should be able to separate the subject from the predicate. The subject is what you are talking about; the predicate offers some sort of comment on the subject. To find the **complete subject** of a clause, ask yourself, "Who or what is doing something?" Include all the words that stick to that *who* or *what*, modifying or specifying it. These words together make up the complete subject. Thus, in the sentence

> *Many young persons who leave school today are functionally illiterate,*

ask yourself, "Who or what are functionally illiterate?" The answer, of course, is *many young persons who leave school today*, so those seven words form the complete subject.

Next, to identify the **simple subject**, look for the head noun, the one significant noun that all the other words in the complete subject modify. Here the head noun is *persons*, and it is the simple subject. You often need to be able to locate the simple subject to know whether its verb should be singular or plural.

The subject we just looked at is a noun phrase, a head noun with all its attached modifiers. This is perhaps the most frequent kind of subject, but other grammatical units can also function as subjects of clauses. What follows is a complete list of subject fillers.

1. Nouns.
   a. Simple noun.
      Honesty is the best policy.

   b. Noun phrase.
      Some of the brighter students asked questions.

2. Pronouns.
   They refused to quit.

3. Nominals.
   a. Adjective.
      Rich and poor alike feared the plague.

   b. Prepositional phrase.
      Before sunrise is too early to start.

   c. Present participle.
      Reading maketh the full man.

   d. Participial phrase.
      Reading the Sunday paper takes two hours.

   e. Infinitive.
      To play is more fun than to work.

   f. Infinitive phrase.
      To play golf well requires practice.

   g. Noun clause.
      That negotiations broke down was unfortunate.

4. Dummy subjects (expletives).

   a. *It.*

   It was unfortunate that negotiations broke down.

   b. *There.*

   There are no available resources.

A **dummy subject** (or **expletive**) is a meaningless and non-referential *it* or *there* filling the subject position of a clause in normal word order so that the true subject can be postponed to follow the predicate. You could, for instance, write *There are two possible answers,* in which *there* is the dummy subject and *answers* is the true subject, rather than *Two possible answers are* [i.e., *exist*].

Except for the dummy subjects, any of these units can be multiplied to form a compound subject. Thus, you might have as a subject *reading and writing* or *cars, ships, and planes.*

Nominals, you recall, are grammatical units that function the same ways nouns do. You can test a suspected nominal by substituting a noun for the nominal. For example, in the sentence *That the negotiations broke down was unfortunate,* replace the noun clause with a simple noun, *the stalemate.* Since *the stalemate* is clearly the subject of *The stalemate was unfortunate,* so too *that the negotiations broke down* must be the subject of the original sentence, in which it fills the noun function and is hence a nominal.

The sentence *That the negotiations broke down was unfortunate* is grammatically correct. Yet it sounds stilted and unnatural. The expletive form of the same sentence, *It was unfortunate that the negotiations broke down,* is the more normal way to handle a sentence with a noun clause as subject. The noun clause is still the <u>true</u> subject, but the dummy subject holds down the beginning subject position, in keeping with correct word order, while the true subject follows the predicate. Some other stylistic reasons for wanting to postpone the true subject might be emphasis, improved rhythm, or a clearer lead-in to the succeeding sentence. Expletives can be overused, and for this reason some critics condemn them as weak and wordy. But like any grammatical construction, dummy subjects are good or bad as they are used wisely or thoughtlessly. The choice—the educated choice—is yours.

11

Noun Modifiers

Since the most common kind of subject is the noun phrase, or the modified noun, we shall look next at the various kinds of modification that can be applied to a noun. Remember that modification makes a word more specific by limiting, changing, identifying, or describing it. Noun modifiers include adjectives and adjectivals, positioned as closely as possible to their head nouns. Here are examples of the different types of noun modifiers:

1. Adjectives.
   a. A single adjective.
      *the **long** trial*

   b. Two or more adjectives before the head noun.
      *the **long, complex** trial*

   c. Two or more adjectives following the head noun.
      *the trial, **long and complex***

   d. Two or more adjectives at the beginning of a sentence, when the head noun is a subject.
      ***Long and complex**, the trial. . . .*

2. Adjectivals.
    a. Other nouns.
        *the **business** executive*

    b. Prepositional phrases.
        *the dust **on the shelves***

    c. Participles
        *the **startling** discovery* (present participle)

        *the **forgotten** citizen* (past participle)

    d. Participial phrases.
        *the nurse **examining the patient***

        *the gun **used in the crime***

    e. Participial phrases at the beginnings of sentences, when the head nouns are subjects.
        ***Examining the patient**, the nurse* . . . .

        ***Used in the crime**, the gun* . . . .

    f. Infinitives.
        *the place **to visit***

    g. Infinitive phrases.
        *the capacity **to feel sorrow***

    h. Relative clauses.
        *the man **who made the speech***

    i. Nominals used as appositives.
        *the bonus, **an unexpected windfall***

A word of caution. Nouns modifying nouns can lead to impenetrable confusion, because the relationship between the nouns is not overt. A *chemistry teacher*, for example, is really a teacher <u>of</u> chemistry; a *college chemistry teacher* is a teacher <u>of</u> chemistry <u>in</u> a college; and a *community college chemistry teacher* is a teacher <u>of</u> chemistry <u>in</u> a college designed <u>for</u> a community. Although this particular four-noun string creates no problem of comprehension, something like *state public water system supervision program grant regulations* (a brainchild of the Environmental Protection Agency) gets downright indigestible. Use noun agglutinations only when they are familiar or easily deciphered, and even then, use them cautiously.

In relative clauses, the relative pronoun is often deleted (omitted) when it is the object of its clause verb. *The experiments that they performed proved useless* could just as clearly be *The experiments they performed proved useless.* Again, *The soprano whom the critics praised won the award* might become *The soprano the critics praised won the award. They performed* and *the critics praised* are still relative clauses; each just lacks a pronoun. The pronoun, in other words, has been deleted. The advantage of deletion is brevity, one less small word to clutter the sentence. The disadvantage, very rarely, is ambiguity. If by any chance omitting the relative pronoun can create confusion, leave it in.

A similar situation exists when the word *that* is used to introduce a noun clause. Though modification is not the issue here, we might as well digress for a moment. A noun clause frequently functions as the object of verbs like *think, know, believe,* or *recognize: Everyone knows that the world is round.* For the sake of brevity, *that* may be deleted: *Everyone knows the world is round.* Nothing has changed; *the world is round* remains a noun clause functioning as the object of the verb *knows.* With truncated, or shortened, noun clauses, however, you run a greater risk of ambiguity. It is quite simple to mistake the <u>subject</u> of the noun clause for the <u>object</u> of the independent-clause verb. For example, *Most students remember the theorem dealing with the square of the hypotenuse was discovered by Pythagorus* can easily be misread, requiring the reader to shift gears and start over. So delete *that* from a noun clause only when you are absolutely certain ~~that~~ your sentence can't be misread.

These instances of a deleted noun-clause *that* or a deleted relative pronoun are the apparent exceptions, mentioned earlier, to the statement that the first word in any dependent clause must be either a subordinating conjunction or a relative pronoun. In Chapter 24 we shall see why the exceptions are merely superficial, in that there is more to these truncated clauses than meets the eye. Until we get to that explanation, however, remember the statement and accept the exceptions. End of digression. Return to modification.

Modification permits you to bring your nouns clearly into focus, to turn the bare name of a thing into a sharply defined, comprehensible reality. Some modifiers are flowery and overly ornate. You probably don't want that kind of modification. But you do want to be specific. Intelligent modification is your tool.

Except for those methods that apply only to nouns as subjects, the kinds of modification discussed in this chapter could work with any noun in any function. Nouns and nominals do not act solely as clause subjects. They can serve other important functions within a clause. We have already noted two main ways that nouns or nominals can function, aside from being subjects: as the object of a preposition—

*Tension can be reduced by **massaging the temples**;*

and as an appositive to an earlier noun—

*The attorney, **a brilliant trial lawyer**, addressed the jury.*

In the next chapter we shall meet two more noun functions, as we dissect the predicate.

12

Clause Predicates

We already know two things about a predicate. We know it is the essential half of a clause, the half that makes some kind of comment about the subject. And we know that it consists of a finite verb form—sometimes, <u>only</u> a verb, as in the tersely moving biblical verse *Jesus wept;* more often, a verb plus certain "optional elements." In the next few pages we shall find out what those optional elements are and what kinds of verbs precede them.

In a sentence having normal word order, the predicate immediately follows the subject. It starts where the subject stops. Whatever is not the subject or a subject modifier is the predicate. To illustrate:

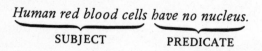

Human red blood cells have no nucleus.

      SUBJECT   PREDICATE

The predicate of this sentence contains the finite verb *have* and a complement, *no nucleus.* A **complement** is a word or group of words that completes the idea expressed by the verb, most often a direct object of the verb. A complement is one of the two larger types of elements optionally found in predicates. The other type is a verb modifier—an adverb or an adverbial.

A **direct object** names something that is affected by the verb's action. In case you are hazy about the difference between a direct object (the most frequent kind of complement) and a verb modifier, take only the subject and verb of a sentence and cast them in the form of a question, with *what, whom, how, when* or *where* as your questioning word. The questioning word that you need differentiates direct objects from modifiers. *What* and *whom* replace direct objects; *how, when,* and *where* replace modifiers. So in the sentence *The dog chewed a bone,* your question would be, **What did the dog chew?** The answer, *a bone,* is the direct object. In another sentence, *The dog growled ferociously,* your question would have to be, **How did the dog growl?** And your answer, *ferociously,* has to be a modifier.†

Though all verbs can be modified, not all can be followed by complements. Verbs can be categorized into three groups by whether they take complements and (when they do) by the kind of complement they require. These groups are called *intransitive verbs, transitive verbs,* and *linking verbs.* They cause students more confusion than they merit.

Both intransitive and transitive verbs indicate actions. But an **intransitive verb** takes no complement. A **transitive verb** does; it must be followed by a direct object. Though this distinction interests grammarians, it has practically no value to writers, because it seldom causes problems. Often a given verb may be both intransitive and transitive, depending on how you use it. Take the verb *to sing.* In *Beverly Sills sings beautifully,* it is intransitive. (*How* does Beverly Sills sing? Beautifully—a modifier.) In *Beverly Sills sings arias,* it is transitive. (*What* does Beverly Sills sing? Arias—the direct object.) Although the distinction is real, knowing the terms will not improve your

---

†If the answer to a *what* or *whom* question is a word renaming, identifying, or describing the subject of the clause, it's not a direct object but a predicate noun or a predicate adjective. You'll understand these terms in a moment, when we discuss linking verbs.

writing, for ignorance of them is not likely to lead you into error.

You may err, though, if you don't understand the peculiarities of **linking verbs**. Unlike the other two verb types, a linking verb does not indicate action. Instead, a linking verb indicates the state or condition of its subject. English has only a handful of linking verbs: *to be* and a few others like *to seem, to appear,* and *to become.* Since a linking verb shows no action, it can never be followed by a direct object: there is no action to affect anything. But it does use two other kinds of complements, a **predicate noun** and a **predicate adjective**, that it links directly to its subject. A predicate noun renames or labels the subject: *Coffee is a stimulant.* A predicate adjective describes or modifies the subject: *Coffee is expensive.*

If you bear in mind that linking verbs don't represent actions, you'll avoid the two mistakes commonly associated with them. With no action to affect anything, there can be no direct object of a linking verb. Hence, *That was him* is incorrect, because *him* is the form of *he* used in object positions. And there can be no adverb of manner describing the (nonexistent) action. Hence, *They felt badly about the loss* is also incorrect. Many careful speakers are so conscious of the need for an adverb with action verbs that they over-correct and say *felt badly.* Here, though, *to feel* is another linking verb, indicating a state, not an action. Therefore, no adverb of manner. A linking verb may, however, be followed by an adverb of place—*The car is here*—or by an adverb of time—*The meeting is tomorrow.* Grammar makes fine distinctions.

You were promised two more noun functions in this chapter. The first of these is the use of a noun or a nominal as the object of a verb:

The president signed the new housing bill.

The second is the use of a noun or a nominal as a predicate noun after a linking verb:

Milton's Paradise Lost *is the greatest English epic poem.*

Predicates occasionally have other kinds of elements, with labels like *indirect object, object complement,* and *predicate appositive.* Knowing them is no more necessary than knowing the difference between transitive and intransitive verbs. Once you get the finite verb into your predicate, whatever optional elements you need will follow as the night the day. We shall be using a few of these terms again: *complement, object of a verb, predicate noun,* and *predicate adjective.* So keep them in mind, but don't worry too much about the rest. The only <u>essential</u> element in a predicate is the finite verb. We'll take a further look at it next.

13

Clause Verbs

A finite verb form is the one absolutely essential element of a grammatical English sentence. It is also rather simple to locate. After the subject has been isolated (and in an imperative sentence, such as *Stop!*, there is no explicit subject to isolate), the first word you meet will be either the finite verb or part of a finite verb phrase. Occasionally an adverb may sit between the subject and the verb, as in *The train slowly climbed the grade*, but the verb is still easy to identify.

Because the English verb is both important and complicated, you need a fairly clear grasp of its parts and characteristics. We've already examined a few of these in Chapter 5; we'll look at verb forms in more detail in Chapter 30. The main thing you have to remember has been emphasized often: the verb of a clause, whether it's a simple verb form like *dug* or a verb phrase like *had been digging,* must have a tense marker. It must be finite.

Just as a clause subject can be compounded—*boys and girls*—so too a clause verb can be compounded—*worked and played.*

Sometimes verb phrases are split up by intervening words. Adverbs and negatives can follow the first auxiliary verb of a verb phrase, as in *could easily have been mistaken* or *will not have finished*. Also, the subject wedges in between the first auxiliary and the remainder of the verb phrase in questioning sentences: *Have the books been balanced*? These interrupted verb-phrase formations are so common that you write them almost instinctively. There's no need cudgeling your brains over them.

You might cudgel briefly over phrasal verbs. *Phrasal verb* is a term that sounds enough like *verb phrase* to cause confusion, but the name is more confusing than the concept. A **phrasal verb** is a two-part verb consisting of a basic verb plus a "particle," a little word like *in* or *up*. This new combination means something different from the verb alone. Consider the simple verb *turn*. By adding different particles, you get phrasal verbs with varying distinct meanings: *turn on, turn off, turn over, turn in, turn up,* and so on. Note the different meanings of the verbs and the verbal in this sentence: *As he **turned** the pages of the ledger, he **turned up** new evidence that he **turned over** to the prosecutor before **turning in** for the night.*

The particles in phrasal verbs look like prepositions, but they aren't. The forms are identical, but the functions differ. Two simple examples illustrate the differences: *Turn off the light* and *Turn off the highway*. In the first example, *light* is the object of the phrasal verb *turn off;* in the second, *highway* is the object of the preposition *off*. A particle can often be moved behind the verb object: *Turn the light off*. But a preposition usually cannot be moved directly behind its object: *Turn the highway off* would be wrong. Moreover, phrasal verbs can often be replaced by one-word synonyms, so that *Turn off the light* equals *Extinguish the light*. No one would doubt that *light* is the object of *extinguish*, so there should be no doubt that *light* is similarly the object of *turn off*.

The confusion between prepositions and phrasal-verb particles has helped foster the erroneous belief that you cannot end a sentence with a preposition. This is one of grammar's many baseless superstitions. *Turn the light off* is a perfectly good English sentence—because it ends with a particle rather than a preposition. But even a true preposition can end a sentence: *I forget which person I mailed it to.* Again, this sentence is <u>grammatically</u> correct—though it may be faulted as <u>stylistically</u> weak in certain kinds of writing.

The end of a sentence is a point of relatively heavy emphasis. Because it is the last part to be read, it leaves a strong impact on the reader's mind. So unless you deliberately wish to emphasize the particle or preposition (*I said to turn the light on, not off!*), it may be poor <u>style</u> to end with a feeble little word like *off* or *in* or *to.* This, however, is a question only of style—of choice, of desired effect—and not at all a question of correct grammar.

Now a word about active and passive verb forms. In normal English word order, the subject of a clause is also the agent or the doer of the action specified by the verb. And the object of the verb is the recipient of its action, the thing affected by the action. We can diagram these relationships this way:

SUBJECT	VERB	OBJECT
↓	↓	↓
The judge	*dismissed*	*the witness.*
↑	↑	↑
AGENT	ACTION	RECIPIENT OF ACTION

This type of pattern is called an **active sentence.**

In a **passive sentence,** the subject of the clause is the <u>recipient</u> of the verb's action, and the agent gets demoted to being the object in a prepositional phrase:

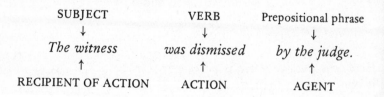

SUBJECT	VERB	Prepositional phrase
↓	↓	↓
The witness	*was dismissed*	*by the judge.*
↑	↑	↑
RECIPIENT OF ACTION	ACTION	AGENT

Or the agent may disappear completely from the sentence:

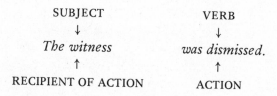

There is another superstition—that we should avoid using the passive, that the active is somehow "better" or "livelier" or "more direct." Not so. The decision to use the active or the passive voice depends upon what you want to do. Usually you want to emphasize the agent, so you put it in the subject spot in an active sentence (for the subject spot at the beginning of a sentence is another position of relative stress). But if you want to emphasize the recipient, put <u>it</u> in the subject spot in a passive sentence. Or if you don't know or don't really care who or what caused the action, omit the agent and again use a passive sentence.

Another consideration in choosing between the active and passive is the continuity of ideas in a sequence of sentences. Look at this sequence:

> *Albert Einstein had one of the greatest minds of all times. He formulated the theory of relativity in 1905 and changed the course of modern physics.*

Here, the active voice is better in the second sentence, for it keeps the focus of attention on Einstein by putting him in the front subject position. But look at this next sequence:

> *The theory of relativity has reshaped modern physics. It was formulated by Albert Einstein in 1905.*

Here, the passive voice is preferable in the second sentence, for it continues to focus on the idea of relativity. Also, on reading these two sequences, we could assume that the first would go on to say more about Einstein and the second would talk further of relativity.

The passive, then, has its advantages. Nonetheless, readers generally expect the subject of a clause to "do" the action of the verb. Therefore, an active sentence is easier to read than is a passive one; it represents the normal way we think. For this reason, you would be wise to choose an active sentence, all other things being equal.

There has been a growing tendency in this century to use the passive voice when it is not really necessary. The tendency is especially noticeable—and deplorable—in bureaucratic writing. This may arise from a desire to ignore or hide the agent of an act. Agents are properly irrelevant in much technical writing, because the focus is on the process: *The ore is heated to 2000° C.* Agents can be embarrassing in politics, because people don't always want credit for their deeds: *Taxes were raised three percent.* No mention of who raised those taxes; the faceless, impersonal passive manages to shuck responsibility for the action. Obviously, this is a bad reason for using the passive. You should use the passive only when you have a good reason. But there are good reasons for the passive. In its proper place, the passive is every bit as effective as the active in its proper place. Once again, the decision involves not grammar, but style—and perhaps ethics. Decide wisely.

It's all right to end sentences with prepositions—judiciously. It's all right to use the passive voice—judiciously. We might as well shatter one more taboo while we're about it. It's all right to split an infinitive. Again, though, be sensible.

A **split infinitive** means that some word or phrase, usually an adverb, intervenes between the *to* and the verb base of the infinitive form: *to frankly assert* or *to more than double.* The "rule" prohibiting such a split is a hand-me-down from Latin grammar. In Latin, an infinitive is one word: *amare* means *to love.* This one word couldn't possibly be split. Some early over-zealous grammarians, thinking that English should resemble

Latin, decreed that English infinitives must never be split—even though good writers have been splitting them for centuries. This, then, is not a rule that accurately reflects language use, but a stricture imposed by misguided scholars. Because English infinitive forms often contain two words (*to assert, to double*), there's no reason why other words can't slip into the middle. But what results should sound normal and readable.

Many people still believe that splitting an infinitive undermines the commonwealth, so you ought to avoid offending them when alternatives are easily at hand. Lengthy and unnecessary interveners are distracting: *The Senate voted to **within the next fiscal year and assuming a normal rise in the gross national product** increase taxes by three percent.* No one can read this monstrosity—but, luckily, few people would write it. Other infinitive splitters may be less murky, but they could still be repositioned with no danger of confused meaning and with perhaps a gain in elegance: *They agreed to **immediately** adjourn* could as easily become *They agreed to adjourn **immediately**.*

Sometimes, however, repositioning an adverb destroys your intended meaning. Consider this example: *They decided to **secretly** investigate building a solar-powered car.* Unless you reframe the entire sentence, the split is demanded here. Any other position of *secretly* changes the sense, making either the decision or the building secret rather than the investigation. In short, don't feel guilty about splitting an occasional infinitive, especially when it beats comfortably on your ear. Strenuous attempts to always avoid splits are unnatural.

14

Verb Modifiers

Just as nouns are modified to make them more specific and informative, so too verbs can be modified. Verb modifiers include adverbs and adverbials, as we see below.

1. Adverbs.
   a. Adverbs of time.

      The man ran yesterday.

   b. Adverbs of place.

      The man ran left.

   c. Adverbs of manner.

      The man ran quickly.

2. Adverbials.
   a. Prepositional phrases.

      The man ran up the hill. (place)

   b. Infinitive phrases.

      The man ran to catch his bus. (manner)

   c. Adverbial clauses.

      The man ran because he was late. (manner)

68

Verb modifiers indicate the time, place, and manner of the verb's action. *Manner* is a rather loose term: it includes reasons, contingencies, exceptions—in fact, any adverbial relationship that does not obviously specify time or place. It just so happens that the three examples of adverbials above indicate one *place* and two *manners*. Infinitive phrases always give reasons (or *manners*) for the verbs they modify. You might think of an adverbial infinitive phrase as implying *in order to: The man ran in order to catch his bus.* The other two kinds of adverbials, however, can modify verbs by time or place or manner.

Grammar books have traditionally said that a dependent clause headed by a subordinating conjunction modifies the main verb in the independent clause; hence, the common name, *adverbial clause*. We can go along with the tradition up to a point, but it doesn't always make much sense. In a case like *The man ran because he was late,* the adverbial clause *because he was late* doesn't modify only *ran*. It tells us as much about the man as about his manner of running. In truth, the whole sentence is what's modified, not merely the verb. *Adverbial clause* is a convenient term, but remember that an adverb can modify a sentence as well as a verb. So you may look upon an adverbial clause as either a verb modifier or a sentence modifier, whichever strikes you as more reasonable. The result's the same.

An interesting feature of adverbs and adverbials is their relative mobility within a sentence. Here are several ways the modifiers in the sample sentences can be combined and shifted about:

> *Quickly, the man ran up the hill.*
> *The man ran quickly up the hill yesterday.*
> *The man quickly ran left to catch his bus.*

Or, using all the modifiers,

> *Yesterday, because he was late, the man quickly ran left up the hill to catch his bus.*

There are many other possibilities in this game. These versions are enough to make the point. Within limits, verb modifiers have fairly flexible positions in the word order of a sentence.

Word order—the positions of words and grammatical units within a clause—is extremely important in English. The normal subject–verb–object order, for instance, is what makes the difference in meaning between *dog bites man* and *man bites dog.* Noun modifiers, you may recall, should always be grouped as closely as possible to their head nouns. Verb modifiers, as we have just seen, are somewhat movable. This distinction influences punctuation as well as sentence arrangement. Before getting into punctuation, though, let's try one more game, this time modifying a noun and verb in the same sentence.

15

Expansion
Through Modification

A thought of any consequence consists of a topic and a comment on that topic. The topic and its comment might be barebones, or they might include additional details, restrictions, explanations, classifications—anything that specifies and defines the basic thought.

A sentence, like the thought behind it, might be a barebones subject-plus-predicate, or it might have added modification to approximate more closely the complex thought it represents. To see how sentences can not only be expanded through modification but also be aligned more closely to reality, consider this flat statement:

Birds fly.

This is as grammatically simple as a sentence can be. It is also a shade simple-minded, for it makes an untrue generalization. The intelligent reader asks, "But what of penguins, ostriches, emus?" So the intelligent writer modifies the sentence, both its subject and its verb, so that it hews more precisely to the facts.

First, let's see what can be done with the subject. What kind of birds have we in mind?

> *Migratory birds* . . .

Any migratory birds? No, just

> *Large migratory birds* . . .

What particular large migratory birds are we interested in?

> *Large migratory birds **living in North America*** . . .

All of them? Not quite:

> ***Most of the** large migratory birds living in North America* . . .

We could continue expanding the modification and narrowing the subject, if we desired. For instance, we could append a list of examples introduced by *such as:*

> *Most of the large migratory birds living in North America, **such as ducks, geese*** . . .

But instead, let's turn to the verb, *fly,* and make it more precise. How do these birds fly?

> *. . . fly **instinctively**.*

Where do they fly?

> *. . . fly instinctively **to warmer climates**.*

When do they fly?

> *. . . fly instinctively to warmer climates **in the declining days of autumn**.*

Again, the modification could be extended, but the adverb of manner, adverbial of place, and adverbial of time should suffice to make the point that modification adds precision to thought. When the full subject and the modified verb are now combined, we have a sentence that has meat on its bones and that accurately reflects reality:

> *Most of the large migratory birds living in North America instinctively fly to warmer climates in the declining days of autumn.*

(*Instinctively* has been shifted in front of *fly* for the sake of rhythm and emphasis—a stylistic choice.)

This is not an unusually long sentence; it consists of just twenty-one words. It could easily be expanded to fifty words and still not be remarkably long. But it is rather interesting in that, despite its length, it is merely a simple sentence—a single independent clause with a single subject, a single predicate, and no dependent clauses.

It is also interesting because it has no internal punctuation. In fact, there is no place in it where a comma could properly be inserted. Usually a sentence of this length needs commas, dashes, or parentheses to guide the reader, showing which words go together and how the various word groups are related. Internal punctuation in a longish sentence also gives the reader a chance to catch his breath. If you try reading the modified bird sentence aloud, you'll find yourself gasping mildly before you reach the period. For this reason, the sentence is a poor one, even though it is grammatically impeccable.

16

Time Out

When you are surrounded by trees, the forest disappears. When you see too many examples, the concepts blur over. This is a good spot to call a time out in order to step back and see what we've been doing.

Basically, a *sentence* is a *subject + predicate*. That's a grammatical definition. Underlying it is a mental process: an *idea* is a *topic + comment*. We think of something—a topic. And we think something about it—a comment. Actually, it's almost impossible to think of a disembodied topic without including a comment. Try to think of *dog* without picturing a brown dog or a large dog or a dog running or some other "commented upon" dog. Topic-plus-comment is really a unit, just as subject-plus-predicate is a unit.

When a mental idea is cast as a grammatical statement, the topic becomes a sentence subject and the comment takes the form either of a predicate (*The dog is brown*) or of a subject modifier (*The brown dog* [*barks*]). You could even say that all commenting is really modification—describing, specifying, limiting, enlarging, or in some other way talking about the topic. Modification, then, is likewise both a mental process and a grammatical reflection of that process.

74

And this is all we have been doing in the last seven chapters—structuring a topic, and a comment upon that topic, and modification of both the topic and the comment. This is what writing a sentence involves.

This is also what writing a paper involves. You have a topic (something that needs writing about) and you have a comment (something that needs to be said about that topic). If you boil this pair down to a single statement, you have the well-known "thesis sentence." If you expand the pair through modification, you have a complete paper. The only difference is that in a sentence, modification uses adjectives and adjectivals, adverbs and adverbials. In a paper, modification uses full sentences and paragraphs. But these larger units are still describing, specifying, limiting, enlarging—that is, modifying—your topic and comment. The concepts are the same, but the arena is wider.

The paradox of modification is that as you expand, you restrict. Our basic sentence of the preceding chapter referred to all birds flying in all possible ways—a vaguely broad generalization. As we expanded the sentence through modification, we restricted its focus to some specific birds flying in some specific ways. The same thing should happen when you write a paper. You take a relatively general thesis and expand it through modification, with definitions, examples, contrasts, explanations, or whatever you need, until you have restricted it to the specific meaning you wish to convey.

Topic and comment; subject and predicate and modification; restriction through expansion. That's what constitutes writing—and thinking.

IV

Grammatical Punctuation

17

A Note
on Punctuation

Two uses of punctuation were mentioned earlier: to show the grammatical relationships between words or groups of words, and to give the reader a chance to breathe. Punctuation has a third function, akin to both of these. In order to understand it, we must digress briefly to examine one difference between writing and speaking.

When you speak, you convey almost as much information by the way you use your voice as by the way you use your words. You let your voice rise or fall. You speed up or slow down. You emphasize certain words by added stress. When you write, you are physically voiceless. Yet you still want your voice to sound through the ink. To some extent, punctuation reproduces the changing voice patterns of speech.

For example, if someone who is speaking to you pauses momentarily and lets his voice hang there . . . , you wait for him to continue. So he says some more words, then pauses again and lets his voice drop. Now you can speak. You know he has finished. Commas and periods do for words on paper the same thing that changing voice contours do for spoken words.

The concept of voice contours helps to illuminate the system of English punctuation. Look at this schematic representation of what is meant by **voice contours**:

Although the trial ended in 1974,   the appeal has not yet been heard.

If you read this sentence aloud, you can notice that your voice maintains a relatively even level until it hits *1974*; then it rises slightly and you pause briefly. Next your voice resumes its original level and stays there until *heard.* Here your voice rises and falls, ending at a lower level than that of the rest of the sentence. And you pause somewhat longer than before (although you need a subsequent sentence to recognize this longer pause). The lines and slashes above the sentence represent these varying voice contours.

Briefly, the contour for a comma is a rise in the original voice level, a slight pause, and a return to and continuation of the original level.

COMMA CONTOUR:

When you hear this contour in speech, you know you need a comma at the up-pause spot in writing. And conversely, if you see a comma, you know there should be an up-pause in your oral reading.

The contour for a period is a rise and fall below the original voice level, a longer pause, and then a continuation of the original level.

PERIOD CONTOUR:

Again, if your voice acts this way—up-down—longer pause—you need a period when you write. Or if you see a period, your voice should follow this contour when reading aloud.

The congruity between voice contours and commas or periods is not absolute. It doesn't always apply to questions or exclamations, for example, or even to all declarative sentences. But it is usually true of normal academic or professional writing. It also provides one more reason for emphasizing that you should always read your writing out loud and listen to your voice. If you hear an up-pause, you should see a comma. If you hear an up-down–longer pause, you should see a period. This system is not foolproof, but it is tremendously helpful.

To return to the sample sentence above, you can see that the comma after *1974* coincides both with the voice contour's rise and pause (where the reader can breathe, if necessary) and also with the end of the dependent clause *although the trial ended in 1974.* That is, the comma separates the words that go together in the dependent clause from those in the following independent clause. This function of punctuation, showing the relationships of words within a sentence, is called **internal punctuation**. The comma is the typical mark of internal punctuation, but dashes and parentheses can replace commas in special situations, as we shall see in Chapter 21.

Again in the sample sentence, the period after *heard* represents both actual voice contour and the end of the sentence. It is an example of **terminal punctuation**. Question marks and exclamation points also occur at ends of sentences, but the period is the usual mark of terminal punctuation.

Internal and terminal punctuation are closely tied to the grammatical structure of a sentence. In the next chapter we shall see various ways to punctuate modified nouns. Then we shall examine the punctuation of modified verbs. And after that, we shall look at other assorted uses of internal punctuation, for it is the internal punctuation that can seem tricky. Terminal punctuation is relatively straightforward. Most writers use question marks instinctively and correctly. Exclamation points hardly ever appear in factual writing, so forget about them. And periods are not too complicated: just remember that they must have at least one independent clause or a deliberate fragment preceding them. That's about all there is to the terminal marks. Now to the internal.

18

Punctuating
Noun Modifiers

We shall approach internal punctuation by looking at the use of commas, first in a modified sentence subject and then in a modified predicate. A noun acting as the subject of a sentence is frequently modified, and this modification may necessitate internal punctuation. Though this chapter shows examples only of modified subjects, in many cases the principles of punctuation demonstrated here also apply to modified nouns serving other functions.

Before getting into the punctuation of sentence subjects, you should keep two points in mind. One, internal punctuation reflects both the voice contours of normal speech and the grammatical relations between words. Two, the normal word order of an independent clause is SUBJECT + PREDICATE.

The subject–predicate combination marks the very existence of a clause. You don't want to split this combination with a comma down its middle. So the first principle of punctuation is simple. Never use a single mark of punctuation between the subject and the predicate. Stress the word *single* here, for there are often times when you will need double marks—say, a pair of commas or a set of parentheses. But never a <u>single</u> mark.

We'll meet two more principles as we work through the

example situations on the following pages. All the examples are based on the same statement, *The judge sentenced the thief.* (Since we are focusing on the subject, the predicate, *sentenced the thief,* will be omitted.) This means that each example represents only one independent clause. Punctuation in a sentence with two independent clauses comes later.

We shall classify noun modifiers according to whether they appear in normal word-order positions or in displaced positions. And if they are in a normal spot, we shall split them again into two groups, those modifiers needing no punctuation and those requiring commas. Notice the importance of the position of the modifying elements in the word order of the sentence. The arrows in the diagrams below show the direction of modification, either forward to the head noun or back to it.

Normal order for subject modifiers, no punctuation needed:

SUBJECT ◄─────── RESTRICTIVE RELATIVE CLAUSE

The judge   *who was hearing the case . . . .*

SUBJECT ◄─────── RESTRICTIVE PARTICIPIAL PHRASE

The judge   *hearing the case . . . .*

SUBJECT ◄─────── PREPOSITIONAL PHRASE

The judge   *on the bench . . . .*

       ADJECTIVE ─────► SUBJECT

The   *stern*   *judge . . . .*

We will talk in a minute about the term *restrictive* and how restrictive modifiers differ from the nonrestrictive modifiers shown next. The point to note here is that, if you read aloud the subjects we have just modified, your voice will remain relatively level. Hence, no punctuation.

> **Normal order for nonrestrictive subject modifiers, punctuation needed:**
>
> SUBJECT ◄────── ❟ NONRESTRICTIVE RELATIVE CLAUSE❟
>
> *The judge*   *, who was a Harvard graduate, ...*
>
> SUBJECT ◄────── ❟ NONRESTRICTIVE APPOSITIVE❟
>
> *The judge*   *, a Harvard graduate, ...*
>
> SUBJECT ◄────── ❟ NONRESTRICTIVE PARTICIPIAL PHRASE❟
>
> *The judge*   *, banging his gavel, ...*

The terms *restrictive* and *nonrestrictive* refer to clauses or phrases that modify a noun. A restrictive clause or phrase gives essential information that must be included in the sentence in order to identify the head noun. The meaning of the sentence would be altered if the restrictive modifier were eliminated. A nonrestrictive clause or phrase, on the other hand, just gives additional information to the reader, something that may be nice to know but that is not absolutely vital. Look at the two examples of participial phrases given above:

> *The judge **hearing the case** sentenced the thief.*
> *The judge, **banging his gavel**, sentenced the thief.*

The first phrase tells exactly <u>which</u> judge did the sentencing; it is essential information. And because it is essential, it must not be separated from its noun by commas. The second phrase adds a touch of action to the statement, but no truly necessary fact. The two commas setting it off show that it is of only incidental interest to its noun and to the sentence. A similar difference can be seen in the two examples of relative clauses: *who was hearing the case* identifies the judge, but *who was a Harvard graduate* is merely peripheral chitchat.

Of course, you can construct a situation in which the Harvard degree is a necessary distinction between that particular judge and another who is a Yale graduate. Indeed, it's sometimes hard to decide logically whether a modifier is restrictive or nonrestrictive.

Consider these two sentences:

> *My next-door neighbors, who love rock music, had a party on their patio last night. People who love rock music shouldn't have outdoor parties.*

The first *who love rock music*, though mildly interesting, is not an essential piece of information; the sentence would communicate its meaning whether the clause were there or not. But the second *who love rock music* is absolutely necessary if its sentence is to make the desired sense. Omit it and you have a totally different meaning that only the most wild-eyed environmentalist could endorse. You might argue that, taking the two sentences in sequence, the first clause is <u>also</u> necessary to their combined meaning. But punctuation is by individual sentences, not sequences. You would just be muddying the water with your logic. Here is where voice contours can help.

If you read these two sentences aloud, your voice will behave something like this:

Your voice clearly reveals the presence or absence of commas. And the point of interest is that your voice would automatically make these distinctions through its contours, even if the punctuation were missing. When you write a sentence and you aren't sure whether you intend the modification to be restrictive or nonrestrictive, read the words out loud and listen. Somehow your voice seems to have a more direct pipeline to your intentions than your "logical" brain does. Your voice can tell you what you mean to say. Follow its contours.

Before returning to the punctuation of sentence modifiers, two more things are worth mentioning. First, you can have restrictive as well as nonrestrictive appositives. An appositive, you may recall, is a word or phrase that renames another noun. Usually appositives are nonrestrictive and require commas, as we saw in *The judge, a Harvard graduate, sentenced the thief.* In the sentence *The poet John Dryden revived classicism in English literature,* however, the appositive *John Dryden* not only renames *the poet* but also identifies which specific poet is being discussed. Hence, it is a restrictive appositive and must not be cut off by commas.

Second, in the "rock music" example, the relative pronoun *that* could replace the *who* of the second sentence, but not of the first. *That* is always a restrictive relative pronoun; it cannot be used in nonrestrictive clauses. Therefore, you should never set off with commas a relative clause headed by *that.* In fact, you might adopt the distinction that all restrictive relative clauses use *that,* with *who* and *which* reserved for nonrestrictive clauses. You need not always observe this practice, but at least refrain from using *that* nonrestrictively.

Often a noun modifier gives no inherent indication that it is restrictive or nonrestrictive. The *that–which* distinction helps with relative clauses, but it is sometimes ignored. With other noun modifiers, only the writer knows whether he wants them to be considered restrictive or not. The one invariable mark of nonrestriction is the presence of commas around a modifier; these commas are the only clue the reader has, or needs. Therefore, when you (or your voice and ear) decide something is nonrestrictive, be careful to set it off by commas. But don't put commas around modifiers that you wish to be read restrictively.

Let's go back now to our basic example, *The judge sen-*

tenced the thief, for there is still one more situation to be considered—the punctuation of a modifying element displaced from its normal word order.

Displaced subject modifiers, punctuation needed:

NONRESTRICTIVE PARTICIPIAL PHRASE **,** ⟶ SUBJECT

Banging his gavel,   *the judge . . . .*
Having heard the case,   *the judge . . . .*

SUBJECT ⟵ **,** ADJECTIVE + ADJECTIVE **,**

The judge   *, stern and humorless, ...*

ADJECTIVE + ADJECTIVE **,** ⟶ SUBJECT

Stern and humorless,   *the judge . . . .*

The punctuation for displaced modifiers warns the reader that some words have been rearranged and shows what words go with what. Further, if you read aloud all those sentence subjects that require punctuation, you will hear your voice rise and pause at each of the indicated commas. So the punctuation also reflects the voice, and the voice reflects the mind at work.

These various ways to punctuate nouns and their modifiers follow three principles. Remember the principles, and you can forget many "rules" of punctuation.

1. Never put a <u>single</u> comma between a subject and its verb.
2. Use no commas with restrictive noun modifiers; set off nonrestrictive noun modifiers with commas.
3. Set off with commas noun modifiers displaced from their normal word order.

Next we shall see how to punctuate verb modifiers in the predicate of our basic example, *The judge sentenced the thief.* The structures differ, but the principles won't change.

19

Punctuating
Verb Modifiers

Punctuating verb modifiers is simpler than punctuating noun modifiers, for there are no restrictive-nonrestrictive distinctions to worry about. Otherwise, the principles are similar. Never put a <u>single</u> comma between the verb and its complement. And set off with commas verb modifiers displaced from their normal word order.

You may recall that, although noun modifiers have to hover near their head nouns, verb modifiers can wander about in the sentence. This permits a few more permutations than were found in positioning noun modifiers. Again, though, normal positions require no internal punctuation.

Normal order for verb modifiers, no punctuation needed:

SUBJECT	ADVERB ——→	VERB	OBJECT
The judge	*reluctantly*	*sentenced the thief.*	

┌─ SPLIT VERB PHRASE ─┐
| SUBJECT | ┌ ◄——— ADVERB ———→ ┐ | | OBJECT |
| *The judge* | *had* | *reluctantly* | *sentenced* | *the thief.* |

SUBJECT   VERB   OBJECT   ADVERB

The judge sentenced the thief   reluctantly.

SUBJECT   VERB   OBJECT   PREPOSITIONAL PHRASE

The judge sentenced the thief   in a quick speech.

SUBJECT   VERB   OBJECT   INFINITIVE PHRASE

The judge cleared the court   to hear the objection.

SUBJECT   VERB   OBJECT   ADVERBIAL CLAUSE

The judge sentenced the thief   because he was guilty.

Notice your level voice contours when speaking these sentences. Notice, too, that you normally don't put verb modifiers between a verb and its object.

As you should expect, verb modifiers that upset the normal word order have to be grouped separately from the rest of the sentence with commas.

Displaced verb modifiers, punctuation needed:

ADVERB,   SUBJECT VERB   OBJECT

Reluctantly,   the judge sentenced the thief.

PREPOSITIONAL PHRASE, SUBJECT VERB OBJECT

In a quick speech,   the judge sentenced the thief.

SUBJECT ,PREPOSITIONAL PHRASE, VERB   OBJECT

The judge   , in a quick speech,   sentenced the thief.

89

INFINITE PHRASE,   SUBJECT VERB OBJECT

To hear the objection,   *the judge cleared the court.*

SUBJECT **,** INFINITIVE PHRASE, ⟶VERB OBJECT

The judge , to hear the objection, cleared the court.

ADVERBIAL CLAUSE   SUBJECT VERB OBJECT

Because he was guilty, the judge sentenced the thief.

SUBJECT **,** ADVERBIAL CLAUSE, ⟶ VERB OBJECT

The judge , because he was guilty, sentenced the thief.

Example sentences often sound stupid, and these are no exceptions. The last two sentences, for instance, are badly ambiguous: they both suggest that the judge, rather than the thief, was guilty. This is a problem in pronoun reference, easily corrected by reordering the pronoun and the noun it replaces:

> *Because the thief was guilty, the judge sentenced him.*
> *The judge, because the thief was guilty, sentenced him.*

Another problem arises in the latter of these sentences. As a general rule, it is wiser not to separate the subject from its verb with a lengthy adverbial, as was done here. The rule derives from common sense and not from grammar, for the sentence is grammatically correct. Your readers, however, may have a problem: by the time they get through the long interposed adverbial and reach the verb, they may have forgotten what the subject was. Long <u>noun</u> modifiers between the subject head noun and its verb cause no trouble, because they are part of the complete subject and hence create no real separation between subject and verb. Verb modifiers are not so closely integral to their verbs as noun modifiers to their nouns, so they do interrupt the subject-verb combination and might cause confusion. Even momentary confusion can be disconcerting. Always make things as easy as possible for your readers.

20

Another Reprise
and a Proviso

The last two chapters illustrated a flock of modifying situations for nouns and verbs, with appropriate punctuation. It may help to stop for a moment and repeat the three principles of modification punctuation, slightly revised to cover both subject and predicate modifiers.

1. Never put a single comma between a subject and its verb or between a verb and its complement.
2. Set off nonrestrictive noun modifiers.
3. Set off modifiers displaced from normal position.

If you understand these principles, you should not be upset by the provisos, the expected exceptions. Punctuation serves a function that has not yet been mentioned, one closely related to the reproduction of voice contours—to wit, the indication of stress or emphasis. The up-pause of a comma inevitably stresses the word before the pause. So if you want to emphasize a word, you can place a comma after it—assuming that the comma is otherwise legal. But if you do <u>not</u> want that emphasis, you may at times omit what would normally be a required comma.

Specifically, the comma might optionally be omitted after an introductory verb modifier if the modifier is relatively brief and contains no verb form within it. Thus, an introductory adverb of time or place (not an adverb of manner, for some reason) or a short introductory prepositional phrase need not be set off by a comma if you feel that omitting it better serves the stress and rhythm that you desire. As a case in point, there is no need for a comma in the sentence *Last week the president held a press conference.* Now compare that sentence with the desired contrastive stress achieved by the use of commas in these two sentences: *Last week, the Dow Jones average rose to 882. This week, it fell drastically to 836.* And as a final example, note the possible ambiguity or misreading that can occur when the comma is unwisely omitted: *In the evening light faded rapidly.*

Here is some practical advice. When preparing your rough draft, adopt the habit of always setting off displaced verb modifiers with commas. Then during revision, if your ear suggests that a comma creates intrusive emphasis or upsets the sentence rhythm, and if you are sure that omitting the comma cannot cause misreading, cross it out.

This same desire for emphasis or rhythm might make a comma desirable before a post-verb modifier even though no comma is needed, normally. In the preceding sentence, for instance, the comma before *normally* is not strictly required. But in this particular case, the comma was deliberately added in order to emphasize the contrast between normal punctuation and the optional punctuation of special stress.

Finally, on very rare occasions it may be a kindness to your readers to insert a comma in one of the *verboten* spots, between a subject and its verb. Such a comma serves to prevent a misreading and should be used only when no alternative is as effective. Never try to straighten out an awkwardly constructed sentence by grafting on a comma. Rewrite the sentence. But a good sentence sometimes requires splitting the subject from its juxtaposed verb. There may be a natural and needed up-pause that the comma reflects and reinforces. When Alexander Pope placed a comma between the subject and the verb in his famous line *Whatever is, is right,* he knew what he was doing.

21

Other
Internal Punctuation

Noun and verb modifiers are not the only elements within a
clause that may need internal punctuation. In this chapter you
will find five more situations where commas or other marks are
required.

PUNCTUATING WORDS
IN A SERIES

A **series** is a group of two or more equivalent grammatical units,
such as *oaks–pines–elms, big–strong, eating–drinking–dancing–
singing,* or *on tables–on shelves–in cabinets.* The punctuation
rule for a series of more than two items is simple:

$$A, \quad B, \quad C, \quad and \; D$$

Thus, we would write *oaks, pines, and elms* or *eating, drinking,
dancing, and singing* or *on tables, on shelves, and in cabinets.*
If the units of the series have their own internal commas, the
units should be separated by semicolons to aid the reader in
sorting things out:

The guests included a banker, John Smith; a surgeon, Mary Jones; and three lawyers, Richard Roe, Jane Doe, and Thomas Brown.

Some people assume that a comma in a series represents an omitted *and;* since *and* appears before the final item in the series, they believe that the last comma before *and* is unnecessary. In fact, though, all commas indicate an up-pause in the voice contour, and this up-pause occurs after *each* series item up to the final one. Listen to your voice as you read this sentence:

Medical science has overcome tuberculosis, typhoid, small-pox, and polio in the last hundred years.

Only *polio,* the final series item, lacks an up-pause; and where there is an up-pause, there should be a comma. The "comma-and" combination before the final item also tells your readers that the series is about to close, thus reducing any chance of their misreading your sentence.

This comma before the final *and* is often called the **series comma.** Despite the logic behind its function, current writers are fairly evenly split over using it. Much printed material that you read will lack a series comma, because of a deliberate policy of omission on the authors' or publishers' part. Yet even those people who usually avoid a series comma are forced to insert one in certain situations, in order to prevent misunderstanding. If the colors of sweaters in a catalogue were listed as *red, white and green and tan,* what color choices could you order? A red sweater? A white one? A red, white, and green one? A white and green one? A green and tan one? A tan one? Only a properly placed series comma can answer these questions. The writer who prefers not to use a series comma must remember to put one in whenever clarity demands it. The writer who automatically uses a series comma doesn't have to stop and weigh each series for clarity. The series will always be clear.

A special series situation arises when two or more adjectives precede the same head noun. Ordinarily, a series of only two units is simply joined by *and: books and papers.* Two adjectives in series before a head noun, though, often use a comma instead of *and:* you could write *a bright and shiny face,* but you would more likely write *a bright, shiny face.* Even though *and* is omitted, however, the comma is not automatically inserted. If each adjective equally modifies the noun, a comma separates the adjectives: *a big, red, juicy apple.* But if the modification is <u>not</u> equal, no commas appear.

Think back to the "birds fly" sentence. In the noun phrase *large migratory birds,* we need no comma between *large* and *migratory,* because these two adjectives are not equivalent: they do not modify the same element and hence are not truly in a series. *Migratory* modifies or restricts *birds,* creating the phrase *migratory birds,* a subclass of all birds in general. *Large,* in its turn, modifies this subclass, *migratory birds.* It is not a second adjective describing *birds,* equivalent to *migratory.* So *large* and *migratory* do not form a series; and where no series exists, there is no series comma. In contrast, the phrase *large, noisy birds* does need a comma, since both *large* and *noisy* equally modify *birds.*

This distinction is sometimes in the eye of the writer, but it nonetheless exists. And as the writer, you can control the distinction by adding or omitting commas. Once again, your voice can be your guide. If you are unsure whether a comma is needed, read the sentence aloud, first making an exaggerated up-pause between the adjectives, then keeping your voice flat, and decide which way sounds right. If the up-pause comma contour does not change the sense, a comma should be used. But if the up-pause sounds inappropriate, a comma would be wrong. So omit it.

SETTING OFF
PARENTHETICAL WORDS

The term **parenthetical words** refers to words that can be omitted from a sentence without distorting or destroying its meaning. If it occurs to you that nonrestrictive noun modifiers are parenthetical words, you are right. Any information included within a sentence as merely incidental but nonessential explanation qualifies as parenthetical.

Despite the name, parenthetical words need not be set off by parentheses, although they may be. The stress or emphasis function of punctuation gets applied here. Parenthetical words are set off by commas, dashes, or parentheses, depending on the amount of attention you want the words to receive. Commas imply normal stress, neither more nor less than what the whole sentence gets. Dashes work like a special proclamation: "Now hear this!" And parentheses are like a whispered aside on the stage, with muted stress. So the choice of punctuation is as follows:

Normal emphasis	... , PARENTHETICAL WORDS , ...
More emphasis	...━PARENTHETICAL WORDS━ ...
Less emphasis	... (PARENTHETICAL WORDS) ...

You can see now that some of the commas demonstrated in the chapters on noun and verb modification could be replaced by dashes or parentheses, if your purpose requires modulated emphasis.

(Dashes are also used, non-emphatically, to set off parenthetical words that have their own inner commas, such as, *None of the three possible courses of action—retreating, moving ahead, or standing firm—seemed attractive.* The dashes here clearly mark the limits of the parenthetical appositive and eliminate confusion with the series commas. Finally, parentheses are also used to enclose larger chunks of incidental information, such as this paragraph.)

SETTING OFF A FINAL APPOSITIVE

A nonrestrictive appositive is one kind of parenthetical expression. Within a sentence, the desired stress determines its punctuation. But if the appositive ends the sentence, you can choose from a different trio of marks, depending partly on stress or emphasis and partly on the level of formality in your writing. In a sentence like *Only one thing was missing   money,* place before the appositive *money* whichever of the following marks best suits your need:

Normal emphasis   Independent clause **,** APPOSITIVE ●

Only one thing was missing, money.

Emphatic, informal   Independent clause ▬▬ APPOSITIVE ●

Only one thing was missing—money.

Emphatic, formal   Independent clause **:** APPOSITIVE ●

Only one thing was missing: money.

INTRODUCING A LIST

A list is merely a special type of final appositive. Like any final appositive, a list must follow a full independent clause. Because a list is by its nature a formal enumeration of items, it is introduced by the formal colon.

Independent clause **:** LIST ●

Thus, you might write, *We need the following supplies: ink, staples, paper clips, and erasers.* The list functions as an appositive, renaming and specifying the noun *supplies.* You should not write, *We need: ink, staples, paper clips, and erasers.* In this second sentence, *ink* is the first of a series of direct objects of the verb *need.* And you never have a <u>single</u> mark of punctuation between a verb and its object, especially not a strong interrupter like a colon. Simply write, *We need ink, staples, paper clips, and erasers.*

SETTING OFF ABSOLUTE ELEMENTS

An absolute construction, you may remember, is a noun–participle or noun–adjective combination that has only a general and tenuous relation with the independent clause to which it is attached. Absolutes are always set off by commas, wherever they appear in a sentence.

ABSOLUTE**,**   SUBJECT   PREDICATE ●

His fingers twisting nervously, the man begged for mercy.

SUBJECT   **,** ABSOLUTE**,**   PREDICATE ●

The man, his fingers twisting nervously, begged for mercy.

SUBJECT   PREDICATE   **,** ABSOLUTE ●

The man begged for mercy, his fingers twisting nervously.

With absolutes, you can once again play the emphasis game. Use dashes if you wish to highlight the absolute: *The battered frigate—her guns signalling victory—limped slowly into port.* Use parentheses if you wish to mute it: *The picnic will be held on Saturday, May 25th (weather permitting).* Just be sure the absolute is somehow clearly separated from the rest of the sentence.

22

Joining
Independent Clauses

All the internal punctuation we have been examining occurs within the borders of a single clause (whether independent or dependent) or of a modified sentence having but one independent clause. Sometimes you want to take two or more independent clauses and join them into one typographical sentence. When you do this, what would have been terminal punctuation at the end of a clause changes to internal punctuation within the new long sentence. There are only four ways this can be done. The diagrams that follow illustrate these four permissible ways to join independent clauses.

The usual link between independent clauses is a coordinating conjunction, combined with or replaced by a comma, a semicolon, or a colon. In the diagrams, the periods at the ends of the independent clauses represent any mark of terminal punctuation—a period, a question mark, or an exclamation point. However, the terminal mark that changes must almost always be a period. The capitalized AND stands for any coordinating conjunction—*and, but, or, nor, for, so,* or *yet.* And the capitalized HOWEVER could be any transitional unit—

therefore, moreover, alternatively, etc. Here are the units to be combined:

Independent clause●   Independent clause●

Obviously, independent clauses can be punctuated as separate typographical sentences, as they are here. To combine them into a single typographical sentence while keeping them both independent, we have four options. You will find examples of the four in the sentence immediately following each diagram.

1. Independent clause**,** AND independent clause●

This is the most common way to join two independent clauses, and it is also the easiest.

2. Independent clause with internal commas ● AND independent
   clause●   **;**

If either independent clause, or both, contain more than one internal comma, it avoids confusion to replace the joining comma with a semicolon; and the semicolon also clearly marks the limits of each clause.

3. Independent clause ● independent clause ●
                     ;

Use the semicolon if you choose to omit the coordinating conjunction; keep an eye, though, on the troublesome case of HOWEVER. When HOWEVER introduces one of the independent clauses, a correctly punctuated sentence reads:

Independent clause ● HOWEVER**,** independent clause●
                   ;

Because there is no coordinating conjunction, a semicolon joins the independent clauses; therefore, this is actually still option 3. But the transitional unit often causes problems. Some people think it is a conjunction that needs only an added comma to link the two clauses: *The referendum seemed popular, however, the voters turned it down.* (The asterisk, remember, marks an unacceptable sentence.) Words like HOWEVER are not conjunctions. They are adverbs. Although they show a relation between the ideas of two clauses, they cannot hold independent clauses together grammatically.

4. Independent clause **:** independent clause **.**

All joined independent clauses should have closely connected ideas: they should be more integrally related than ideas in successive sentences. The colon is used only with certain specific relations, ones in which the second clause either defines, restates, or illustrates the idea of the first clause.

A few comments are in order. If the clauses in option 1 have very closely connected ideas and if both clauses are relatively short, the comma may be omitted. You could choose to write, for example, *The wind roared and the thunder crashed*—no comma. Use this stylistic choice carefully. You may end up with a loose, meandering sentence otherwise.

Similarly, but even less frequently, if the clauses in option 3 are short and quite close in structure, you might substitute a comma for the semicolon. Thus, *I came, I saw, I conquered.* This stylistic device is highly unusual and can be dangerous. If your intention is not obvious, readers will view such sentences as having *comma splices*—that is, commas ineffectively and incorrectly holding clauses together. And a nondeliberate comma splice is a serious writing gaffe.

There is, however, one situation that quite normally calls for a comma splice. This situation requires a negative statement in the first clause. The second clause then either makes a contrast with the first clause (*He was not a tiger, he was a pussycat*) or restates the idea of the first clause with a greater degree of emphasis (*The experiment was not merely a failure, it was an utter fiasco*). These particular comma splices occur fairly infrequently, but they are nonetheless correct. Actually, they are a "correct option," because a semicolon could be (but usually isn't) used.

One more point merits discussion. You probably know that a comma goes in front of a coordinating conjunction and not behind it (*He stumbled, but he won* and not *He stumbled but, he won*). Nor does a comma follow a subordinating conjunction. In fact, we could add a new rule to our list of punctuation principles: Never put a <u>single</u> comma after any conjunction. Sometimes, though, a writer feels a need for the emphasis of a pause after a coordinating conjunction, especially when that conjunction heads a new sentence. Perhaps he writes, *Guns are used for sport and self-defense. *But, guns are also used in crimes.* He wants to stress the contrast. The stress is gained, but at the price of an incorrect comma.

He could achieve the same stress correctly by one of several ways. He could start the second sentence with a synonymous transitional adverb, which is usually set off by a comma anyway: *However, guns are also used in crimes.* He could begin with an adverb of manner: *Unfortunately, guns are also used in crimes.* Or he could insert a parenthetical phrase between *but* and *guns,* providing the desired stress through a permissible <u>pair</u> of commas: *But, in too many cases, guns are also used in crimes.* You can usually find alternative ways in English to make your point effectively. Don't settle for an erroneous choice.

You may recall from early schooling three terms for sentences: *simple, compound,* and *complex* (plus the hybrid variety, *compound–complex*). So you may be wondering why these terms don't appear in this book. They don't appear (except here) because they are unnecessary and misleading. They are unnecessary because it is just as easy (and probably clearer) to describe a sentence as having only one independent clause rather than *simple,* or two independent clauses rather than *com-*

pound, or one independent and one dependent clause rather than *complex,* or whatever other combination it might have. And the terms are misleading because *simple* suggests easy or babyish, and *complex* suggests complicated or difficult. *Compound,* in turn, suggests two or more parts put together—like a complex sentence, maybe?

Let's look at these labels in action, to see just how much light they shed. Consider this pair:

> *He worked overtime, for he needed the money*—compound.
> *He worked overtime, because he needed the money*—complex.

If that wasn't helpful, look at this trio:

> *After work, he relaxed*—simple.
> *After finishing work, he relaxed*—again, simple.
> *After he finished work, he relaxed*—complex.

Finally, here is a slightly far-fetched but accurately labeled example, with a paired sentence:

> *The phenomenon involving the atmospheric precipitation of hydrogen oxide in its liquified form has as an invariable concomitant a torrential deluge of impressive magnitude*—simple.
> *When it rains, it pours*—complex.

Case closed.

V

Cutting
and Pasting

23

Combining
Clauses

You've just seen several ways to combine two independent clauses (or sentences) into one longer typographical sentence, both the clauses remaining independent. A more common way to combine clauses is to **reduce** one of the clauses to a subordinate status. It might become a dependent clause or some type of phrase; in any case, it turns into a modifier of the remaining independent clause. You have your choice among a variety of methods of reduction (subordination). Here's where the fun of grammatical juggling enters in.

Let's start with two independent clauses and see what can be done to join them. They are distinguished by one's being boldfaced:

Caesar crossed the Rubicon.
Caesar marched on Rome.

Now we will look at just a few of our options.

1. *Caesar crossed the Rubicon, and **he marched on Rome**.*

Here, the only change has been to use a pronoun to replace

Caesar in the second clause. We still have two independent clauses connected by the standard **,** AND link.

> 2. *After Caesar crossed the Rubicon, he marched on Rome.*

The original first clause is now an adverbial dependent clause, introduced by the subordinating conjunction *after.*

> 3. *Caesar marched on Rome after crossing the Rubicon.*

Now the original first clause has been reduced to a participial phrase. The phrase functions as the object of the preposition *after* in an adverbial prepositional phrase.

> 4. *Caesar marched on Rome after his crossing of the Rubicon.*

In this version, the original first clause has become merely a nominal phrase, the object of *after* in another adverbial prepositional phrase. Notice that the nominal phrase, *his crossing of the Rubicon,* contains its own included prepositional phrase, *of the Rubicon.* Circles within circles.

> 5. *Caesar, who marched on Rome, first crossed the Rubicon.*

The original second clause has been changed to a relative clause. This dependent clause modifies *Caesar,* the subject of the independent clause. The word *first* has been added to show the time sequence of the two events, just as *after* was added earlier and *then* will appear in the next combination.

> 6. *Caesar, who crossed the Rubicon, then marched on Rome.*

Just for variety, the original <u>first</u> clause has been reduced to a relative clause.

7. *Crossing the Rubicon,* **Caesar marched on Rome.**

The original first clause is again a participial phrase, as in example 3, but the phrase is now an adjectival modifying *Caesar.* Notice that the verbal *crossing* has an implied subject, Caesar, the person who did the crossing—the same subject that appeared in the original full clause, before reduction. This implied subject is identical to the noun in the independent clause that the verbal modifies. We can see that a participial phrase used as an adjectival is somewhat like a sentence that has "lost" its subject. When the phrase heads a sentence, it must borrow as its subject the first noun it finds in the independent clause to which it's hooked. The first noun is usually the subject of the independent clause, as in example 7.

What all this means is that the stated subject of the independent clause must do double duty as the implied subject of the participial phrase. If the two subjects are not the same, you run into trouble. Suppose that the sentence in example 7 had read **Crossing the Rubicon, Rome became Caesar's goal.* Here, the subject of the independent clause, *Rome,* must also function as the implied subject of the participial phrase, so that you have Rome doing the crossing. Such an error is called a **dangling modifier,** because the participial phrase, which should find its implied subject in the nearest noun, has no reasonable adjacent noun to attach itself to. It just dangles.

8. *The Rubicon having been crossed,* **Caesar marched on Rome.**

In this example, the original first clause has been reduced to a neat, concise, and somewhat self-contained absolute, connected to the entire second clause rather than modifying any of its specific words.

Enough of Caesar. Other combinations are possible, but these suffice to suggest the wide range of options at a writer's disposal. Let's try combining two different sentences, concentrating this time on relative (adjectival) clauses. Again, the fact that one is boldfaced serves only to differentiate the two sentences.

> *The lawyer was an expert in torts.*
> *The lawyer tried the case.*

We have four choices for combining these sentences through the use of relative clauses that are then reduced further.

> 9. *The lawyer **who tried the case** was an expert in torts.*
> 10. *The lawyer **trying the case** was an expert in torts.*

In example 9, the original second sentence has become a restrictive relative clause. In example 10, this relative clause has been further reduced to a restrictive participial phrase.

> 11. *The lawyer, who was an expert in torts, **tried the case**.*
> 12. *The lawyer, an expert in torts, **tried the case**.*

Here, the original <u>first</u> sentence has been turned into a <u>non</u>restrictive relative clause and then, in example 12, has been reduced again to an appositive, by deleting *who was*. Whenever you write a nonrestrictive relative clause opening with *who* or *which* and having a form of *to be* as its verb, consider the possibility of a tauter, more concise appositive.

Another demonstration. Here is a similar pair of sentences, but the first sentence has predicate adjectives rather than a predicate noun.

The lawyer was young and inexperienced.
The lawyer tried the case.

Once again, we shall reduce each sentence in turn to a relative clause and then to a phrase.

13. *The lawyer **who tried the case** was young and inexperienced.*
14. *The lawyer **trying the case** was young and inexperienced.*

These examples resemble precisely examples 9 and 10.

15. **The lawyer**, *who was young and inexperienced,* **tried the case.**
16. **The lawyer**, *young and inexperienced,* **tried the case.**

As in examples 11 and 12, the original first sentence has been turned into a nonrestrictive relative clause, and then *who was* has been deleted in example 16, leaving an adjectival appositive. Note that you can't make this deletion with a <u>restrictive</u> relative clause. If the fact of the lawyer's youth and inexperience serves to distinguish him from a second lawyer, the relative clause must remain complete and "uncommaed":

The lawyer $\begin{Bmatrix} who \\ that \end{Bmatrix}$ *was young and inexperienced tried the case.*

When an appositive is formed with adjectives, we have one more possibility for juggling the words.

17. *Young and inexperienced, the lawyer tried the case.*

The appositive adjectives of example 16 have been repositioned to the head of the sentence, set off from *the lawyer* with a comma.

18. *The young, inexperienced lawyer tried the case.*

In this final example, the first sentence has become merely a pair of adjectives, placed between *the* and *lawyer* according to normal word order and separated from each other by a comma because they both equally modify *lawyer.*

We could keep up these shiftings and changes with many other examples. For instance, the whole range of adverbial relations has been somewhat ignored, as in *Although the lawyer was young and inexperienced, he tried the case* or *Despite his youth and inexperience, the lawyer tried the case*. Nor have we used passive variations, like *The case was tried by the young, inexperienced lawyer*. The examples given above, then, are by no means a complete catalogue of ways to combine sentences. They only serve to remind you of the multiplicity of patterns available to you as you put your ideas together on paper.

In this chapter we've been building longer sentences from two shorter sentences. In the next chapter we'll reverse the process, taking a longer sentence and dissecting it into its components. The more angles from which you examine a thing, the better your odds of understanding it. After that, we'll move up the ladder a step to figure out how we can tie two or three sentences together to build a sequence of coherent prose. That gets pretty close to real writing. To anticipate those chapters somewhat, we ought first to consider one more question that arises from the sentence-combining patterns shown in this chapter.

How do you decide which of these patterns to use? If you consider a sentence in isolation, there is no way to label one pattern as better or worse than another. Nor can you tell which of two clauses should be kept independent and which should be reduced. Everything depends on the context in which the sentence will appear. What preceding words lead into the sentence?

What idea should receive the focus? Where will the discussion move in the next sentence? What earlier patterns do you want to echo, or to avoid? These are the kinds of questions that influence your combination of clauses. The sample sentences that we have been playing with are devoid of context and hence are neither good nor bad. They merely show you how clauses can be combined grammatically. But which method you pick in a given instance depends on the totality of your writing. There are no rules and few guides, because each situation differs.

Therefore, experiment. Don't stick monotonously to any small handful of patterns. Expand your repertoire. Widen your options. English affords very precise ways to make connections between ideas, but you can't use them if you don't know them. By now, you should know them.

24

A Peek
Underneath

In the preceding chapter we took two simple sentences and packed them into one sentence by changing the grammatical structure of one or the other of them. Another way to consider this is to say that we took one long sentence and split it into its two simpler components. Any sentence that exceeds a flat "subject + verb + object" structure has simpler sentences underlying it.

To see what this means, let's examine an apparently quite simple sentence: *The large dog chewed a bone.* Here we have the subject + verb + object structure. But we also have an adjective. Is this easy sentence really the result of combining two even simpler sentences? Yes. Underneath it we could find these primer sentences:

The dog was large.   +   The dog chewed a bone.

The primer sentences are called **base sentences**. Their combined form, *The large dog chewed a bone,* is called a **surface structure**, for it is the structure we would usually see in print—unless we were looking at a first-grade reader, in which base sentences might always appear as surface structures. More often, base sentences lie underneath the surface structure, vaguely implicit, in what is called the **deep structure** of a sentence.

These concepts come from transformational grammar, one of the more recent models designed to describe and explain the intrinsic grammar of a language. Some of the ideas suggested by this new grammar offer enlightening clues to how sentences work.

Transformationalists were struck by the similarities in sentences like these:

> *John has eaten his dinner.*
> *John has not eaten his dinner.*
> *Has John eaten his dinner?*
> *After John has eaten his dinner, he will . . . .*
> *Having eaten his dinner, John will . . . .*

They realized that all these sentences have in common the same base sentence, *John has eaten his dinner,* and that the four "different" surface structures merely represent this base sentence **transformed** through added words or repositioned words or modified grammatical structures with deleted words. The grammatical system was named for these transformations.

A strict transformationalist would argue that *John has eaten his dinner* is not a base sentence at all, because it contains at least two deeper structures: *John has eaten dinner + John has a dinner.* Further, these could be dissected into even "baser" propositions. But there is no need for us to seek such precision because, though we can profitably borrow the concepts of transformational grammar, we shall apply its terms rather imprecisely. For our purposes, a base sentence is any sentence that can be constructed from part of a surface structure. And a surface structure is any sentence that contains shorter base sentences within it, either complete base sentences or transformed base sentences.

It should be obvious that we could have used our version

of the term *base sentence* for any of the pairs in the last chapter—say,

> *The lawyer was an expert in torts.*
> *The lawyer tried the case.*

Then any of the combined versions—say, *The lawyer, an expert in torts, tried the case*—would be a *surface structure*. In this example, we would say that the base sentence, *The lawyer was an expert in torts*, is **embedded**, in the form of an appositive, inside the other base sentence, *The lawyer tried the case.*

Turning the process upside down, we could say that any appositive represents an embedded base sentence. So when we see a surface structure that has an appositive, like *The piston rod, a metal bar about ten inches long, connects to the crankshaft*, we can recognize two base sentences: *The piston rod is a metal bar about ten inches long*, sentence one, embedded inside *The piston rod connects to the crankshaft*, sentence two. Notice that the subject of the embedded sentence is identical to a noun in the other base sentence and that the subject and the verb of the embedded sentence have been deleted in the surface structure. This really approximates a grammatical definition of an appositive—an embedded base sentence with a deleted subject and verb, in which the subject is identical to a noun in the receiving base sentence.

You may recall what was said in the previous chapter about avoiding dangling participles: the participial phrase must have the same "implied subject" as the subject of the independent clause to which it is attached, since it has "lost" its own subject and must "borrow" from the clause. We can now state all this more precisely. A participial phrase represents an embedded base sentence. In the surface structure, the subject of the embedded sentence is deleted and the verb is changed to a present or past participle. This can be done only if the deleted subject is identical to the noun it modifies in the receiving sentence. Thus, the surface structure *Approaching the river, the platoon hit an ambush* has in its deep structure two base sentences with identical subjects: the receiving sentence *The platoon hit an ambush* and the embedded sentence *The platoon was approaching the river.* The subject and the auxiliary verb of the embedded sentence are deleted. The result: a proper participial phrase.

If you are checking your rough draft and happen to note two short sentences with repeated nouns, at least one of which is the subject of its sentence, you might decide to combine them through the use of a participial phrase. You can do this by deleting the "subject" noun and changing its verb to a present or past participle. Then merely attach the participial phrase to the retained noun as a modifier.

Observe that we have emphasized the participial phrase at the front of a sentence, where it modifies the subject of the independent clause. The reason is that this is the only place where the participial phrase can be repositioned and hence the only place that can cause trouble. All other participial phrases follow their head nouns in normal word order, so there is no possibility of a dangling modifier.

Suppose you embed a sentence to make it modify the object of a verb, rather than the subject. When you take the base sentence *In 1964 Congress passed a bill* and embed in it a second base sentence, *The bill expanded civil rights*, you simply delete the repeated noun (and its article) and change the verb *expanded* to the present participle *expanding*. Then you attach the resulting participial phrase immediately behind the noun it modifies: *In 1964 Congress passed a bill expanding civil rights.* This kind of situation never creates a problem of dangling. Maybe that's why grammar books seldom discuss it.

An *absolute* is another instance of a base sentence's being transformed and grafted onto a second sentence. An absolute was described earlier as a noun–participle or noun–adjective combination, loosely associated with an independent clause. One example given was *Congress having adjourned, the representatives went home to their districts.* More accurately, we can now define an absolute as a subject–participle or subject–adjective combination, for an absolute is derived from a partially deleted base sentence. In the example above, *Congress having adjourned* is the absolute, and *Congress had adjourned* is its base sentence. In the absolute, the verb is transformed into a present participle (*having adjourned*); but the subject (*Congress*) is retained, for only repeated elements may be deleted, and there is no noun, *Congress,* in the independent clause. Similar reasoning explains *His voice firm, the accused pled "not guilty."* The absolute—*his voice firm*—derives from the base sentence, *His voice was firm.* The linking verb is deleted and the retained subject–adjective combination is attached to the independent clause, *the accused pled "not guilty."*

The concept of base sentences and transformed surface structures also casts light on the reversal of nouns in active and passive sentences. You may recall that an object in an active sentence becomes the subject of its passive version. You may further recall that the normal word order of a clause is subject + verb + object. This means that an active sentence is a "normal" basic form, so that every passive sentence must be derived from an active base sentence in its deep structure. And this in turn explains why the deep-structure object (*The boy kicked the ball*) remains the "objective" recipient of the verb's action even when it becomes the surface-structure subject (*The ball was kicked by the boy*).

Finally, you may remember the comment in Chapter 9 that dependent clauses must always start with subordinating conjunctions or relative pronouns, apparent exceptions notwithstanding; and you may have wondered when we would explain this statement. Now is the time. The "exceptions" were the truncated clauses discussed in Chapter 11, such as *The experiments they performed proved useless.* We can now say that the deep structure of this sentence has a full clause headed by a relative pronoun: *The experiments that they performed proved useless.* In fact, the even deeper structure has two base sentences: *They performed experiments* and *The experiments proved useless.* In the embedded sentence, the repeated noun *experiments* is changed to the relative pronoun *that,* repositioned in front of the subject, and the resulting relative clause *that they performed* is embedded in the other base sentence immediately behind the noun it modifies. So the relative pronoun really heads the dependent clause. The fact that it is deleted in the surface structure reflects a stylistic option but does not affect the "presence" of the relative pronoun. Visible or not, a relative pronoun or a subordinating conjunction remains an essential grammatical element in a dependent clause.

This may all sound like a very complicated way to treat garden-variety sentences. Peeking underneath the surface of sentences, however, can give us useful insights into the many ways sentences get plugged into one another. It also provides a handy trick for straightening out a sentence whose parts don't quite mesh. The more intelligent and mature you are, the more you tend to write rather lengthy, complicated sentences. Once in a while such sentences can get out of hand. Should this happen to you, break your trouble-maker into the base sentences that lie in its deep structure. Then try different ways to rearrange these base units until you transform them into a surface structure that hangs together. This method assures that you don't lose your original ideas; you just lose your awkward constructions. And that loss is a gain.

25

Sentences
in Context

Let us assume that by now you are so knowledgeable that all of your sentences will be grammatically correct. Each sentence in isolation will hang together according to an acceptable pattern. But you are also aware by now that most sentences can be cast in an array of acceptable patterns, each one presenting essentially the same idea. How can you pick the best pattern for your sentence?

In isolation, you can't. This was pointed out in the chapter on clause combinations, but it bears repetition. Any grammatical sentence is as "good" as any other grammatical sentence, when it just sits by itself. Context alone can permit "better" or "worse" decisions. We seldom write only a sentence. We write a paragraph, a passage, a paper. A given sentence will be surrounded by a context of other sentences, some leading into it, others stemming from it. The mutual influence of all these sentences upon one another is what guides you in your preference of patterns. Ultimately, though, you base your decisions on the underlying ideas—on what you want to convey, where you want the emphasis to fall, and how you want your ideas to flow.

Several recent investigations into grammar offer suggestive

analogies for this problem of pattern choice. One approach uses a theatrical comparison. Our ideas perform on paper like actors on a stage. Though the cast may be large, each portion of the action tends to focus on one actor at a time. This actor stands center stage, with supporting actors grouped around him and supernumeraries momentarily in the wings. As the focus shifts, another actor is spotlighted, and the earlier star steps back to a supporting role, only to return on cue to the center of focus. So, too, ideas are staged within a series of sentences. The focus may remain on one idea for a time, but when it shifts, the sentence provides a cue, a lead-in, to the next focused idea.

All very well and good. But how do you transfer this analogy of *focus* and *staging* to your writing? A sentence, grammarians suggest, has two points of focus. The primary focus falls at the beginning of a sentence, the part a reader sees first. A secondary yet still strong focus falls at its end, the part a reader sees last. The words or phrases in the middle tend to be overshadowed by these two peaks of attention. One implication is immediately clear: the middle may be the place to tuck any minor restrictions or qualifications you wish downplayed. The optimist writes, *The national economy, unless OPEC raises oil prices, will remain healthy.* The pessimist writes, *The national economy will remain healthy, unless OPEC raises oil prices.* The focus makes the difference.

When you want one idea to retain the focus throughout a series of sentences, you stage that idea at the front of each sentence. You can do this by making the idea the subject of each of the sentences, holding to a minimum any introductory words. The passive voice is helpful here, for it makes a surface subject of a deep object. Sentence inversion can be another useful option for getting a focused idea to the front. If the idea must go into a subordinate element (say, an adverbial clause), you can swing the whole clause to the front of the sentence.

As the focus prepares to shift to a new idea, you can construct a transition sentence. The idea currently in focus stays at the front; the new idea occupies the focal spot at the end of the sentence. Here it acts as a cue to its reappearance at the beginning of the next sentence, with the new focus. Or a transition of focus might be a time to choose a dummy-subject construction. If the new idea is the true subject of the sentence, putting a dummy subject in the normal subject position permits you to postpone the "cue" words to the end of the sentence.

In a dummy-subject construction, a noun clause is often the true subject. Such noun clauses should put to rest a traditional writing adage: "Place the main idea in the main clause and the subordinate ideas in subordinate clauses." That may sound reasonable, but it's not always true. It says that main ideas should not appear in subordinate structures. Yet the main idea of the sentence you just read appears in the subordinate noun clause; the <u>main</u> (i.e., independent) clause merely gives the trivial information, *it says.* Don't confuse main ideas with main clauses. A main clause is a grammatical structure. A main idea is whatever you want the focus of your sentence to fall on. Focus can fall with equal ease on main clauses or on subordinated elements. You decide.

A practical demonstration of focus and staging will make these concepts less abstract. Cast your critical eye over the two paragraphs that follow. Both present the same ideas, couched in the same number of sentences and often even in the same words. But the staging varies.

In modern times, people have hailed science as the saviour of mankind, the panacea for all problems. The railroad, the telegraph, the jet plane, and television have united people. Science cured yellow fever and diphtheria. We have better crops, a higher standard of living, and men on the moon, all through science. We could enter a new Eden, we felt, if science were just given sufficient funds and freedom. That science also creates new problems, however, slowly became clear to us. Science produced more food and better medicine, leading to overpopulation. Because of industrial progress, the environment is polluted. The atomic bomb grew from "pure" research. Before we can truly assess science, we have to weigh these disadvantages against the advantages.

Science in modern times has been hailed as the saviour of mankind, the panacea for all problems. Science united people with the railroad, the telegraph, the jet plane, and television. It cured yellow fever and diphtheria. It increased crops, raised the standard of living, and put men on the moon. If science were just given sufficient funds and freedom, we felt, we could enter a new Eden. But it slowly became clear to us that science also creates new problems. Overpopulation springs from more food and better medicine. Environmental pollution results from industrial progress. The atomic bomb grew from "pure" research. These disadvantages must be weighed against the advantages before we can truly assess science.

Neither paragraph will win a Pulitzer. But the first, you will no doubt agree, is worse than the second. It is jerky, incoherent, and confusing. The second has better continuity. It keeps the focus on science throughout the first five sentences. The sixth sentence, with its dummy subject, cues in a switch in focus to the end word, *problems.* The next three sentences focus on examples of problems; then the last sentence switches focus again from the problems (*these disadvantages*) back to *science,* the closing word. Finally, this closing word links to the opening word for reinforced emphasis on the encompassing topic of the paragraph—science.

You might want to try identifying the small adjustments in sentence patterns that make the second paragraph an improvement over the first. Incidentally, all the sentences are grammatical. In another context, a sentence pattern from the first paragraph might work better than its counterpart in the second. But in this context, the patterns in the first paragraph just don't mesh.

Some grammarians prefer to explain sentence continuity through the concept of *old information* and *new information.* Once you present an idea to your reader, it becomes old information. Your next sentence then begins with that old information and expands it with new information. Your third sentence treats this new information as old, adding a different chunk of new information. According to this theory, then, the subject of each sentence after the first presents old information, and the predicate, new information (which becomes old in the subject of the next sentence). You might want to check this concept against a random piece of prose. It often proves true, and it provides one more suggestion for structuring your sentences in context, having the old always leading into the new. If this concept is too slavishly followed, however, you'll have the kind of mechanical links found in the nursery fable: "For want of a nail, a shoe was lost. For want of a shoe, a horse was lost. For want of a horse, a rider was lost. For want of a rider . . . ."

There are any number of ways to build mortises and tenons between your sentences. We will look at another approach to continuity in the next chapter. The point you want to remember is that no sentence pattern is inherently superior to another. It all depends on where it's coming from and where it's going. In an appropriate context, even the oft-maligned stringy pattern of clause-*and*-clause-*and*-clause-*and*-clause might prove your most effective choice. You aren't looking for sentences that can stand alone. You want sentences that work together in context, sentences that dovetail.

26

Sentence
Sequences

Written discourse, as we have just seen, does not consist of one sentence, no matter how skillfully crafted. Once you know how to write and punctuate a grammatical sentence, your bigger problem is to build a sequence of related sentences into a coherent chunk of prose.

The solution to this problem moves far beyond grammar proper into other aspects of the writing process. But stringing sentences together to form an intelligent paper involves two grammatically related actions. Here, then, is a grammatical approach to prose coherence.

One: you should be certain that every sentence you write after the opening line has some kind of **grammatical link** to an earlier sentence. It may be a link to the immediately preceding sentence, or perhaps to one several sentences back. The link itself is a more specific connection than the kind of arrangement-of-parts we looked at in the preceding chapter. It might be a pronoun whose related noun appears in an earlier sentence. It might be an introductory coordinating conjunction, a transitional phrase, a key word repeated from a previous sentence, a sentence structure that parallels an earlier structure. Whatever form the link may take, <u>some</u> sort of identifiable link should usually be present. These grammatical connections are almost inevitable between the sentences of a paragraph. But they are not confined within paragraphs: they often occur across paragraph boundaries, linking, perhaps, the closing sentence of one paragraph with the opening sentence of the next.

Two: you should be certain that every sentence that is grammatically linked to a previous sentence also has a clearly apparent **logical relation** with that <u>same</u> sentence. There are only seven significantly important logical relations between sentences. These seven relations can most easily be remembered by the seven key words that represent them: †

AND	a continuation of the same idea with new facts
BUT	a turn or reversal in the idea of the earlier sentence
OR	an alternative for the earlier sentence
THAT IS	a definition or restatement of the earlier sentence
FOR EXAMPLE	an illustration of the earlier sentence
THEREFORE	a conclusion or effect based on the earlier sentence
FOR	a reason or cause for the earlier sentence

Of course, this does not mean that every sentence will start with a key word like *and* or *but* or *therefore* or with one of their many synonyms (*moreover, likewise; conversely, still; thus, hence,* etc.). Quite often, the logical relation between sentences is implied rather than stated. But it does mean that the relation should be present and should be obvious enough to be easily inferred by your readers.

Check your writing. If you do not have grammatical links between pairs of sentences, if you do not have readily discernible logical relations between those same two sentences, then your ideas may seem disconnected and your writing disjointed. Good prose consists of chained sentences, linking down

---

†Adapted from Louis T. Milic, *Stylists on Style* (New York: Charles Scribner's Sons, 1969), p. 21.

and back, the second to the first, the third to the second, the fourth to the third, the fifth perhaps back to the second, the sixth to the fifth, and so on throughout a well-knit paper. If your own sentences don't hold together, add the missing grammatical links and clarify the fuzzy logical relations until you get a chain of ideas that can't be misunderstood.

VI

Styling
Your Sentences

27

Parallelism

Little mention has been made so far of the fourth essential rule of grammar: **Coordinating and correlative conjunctions must join equal grammatical units.** Yet whenever a sentence has any duplicated elements in it (and many sentences do), this rule keeps the pieces properly parceled out. Coordination is directly connected with another important concept of grammar—parallelism.

Parallelism can be defined as the repetition of equal units in similar structures having similar functions. The concept of parallelism rejects *The novel is selling briskly and a critical success*, with part of a verb phrase paired incorrectly with a noun phrase, but accepts *The novel is a best seller and a critical success*, with two parallel noun phrases, both functioning as predicate nouns. The concept also accepts *He reads the books, the journals, and the reports in his field*, with *the* repeated before each noun, or *He reads the books, journals, and reports in his field*, with the first *the* by implication extending to the other two parallel nouns. However, it rejects *He reads the books, journals, and the reports in his field*. The touchstone here is consistency.

Parallelism within a sentence can most easily be visualized

if you uncover the base sentences underneath the surface structure. In the second of the examples just cited, you would find three base sentences, all structurally parallel with one another:

> *He reads the books in his field.*
> *He reads the journals in his field.*
> *He reads the reports in his field.*

You can then delete whatever repetitions you decide are not needed, but you have to be consistent in the deletions. In the first acceptable version, the deletions look like this:

> *He reads the books ~~in his field~~.*
> *~~He reads~~ the journals ~~in his field~~.*
> *~~He reads~~ the reports in his field.*

Then you insert two commas and an *and* to complete the surface structure. In the second acceptable version, the deletions go just a bit further:

> *He reads the books ~~in his field~~.*
> *~~He reads the~~ journals ~~in his field~~.*
> *~~He reads the~~ reports in his field.*

In both of these versions, two sets of identical words were deleted from the base sentences. But in the rejected version, one of the sets of deletions was <u>not</u> identical, as we can see:

> *He reads the books ~~in his field~~.*
> *~~He reads the~~ journals ~~in his field~~.*
> *~~He reads~~ the reports in his field.*

When you write, it is a simple matter to reconstruct in your mind the base sentences that underlie any coordinated series appearing within a clause. Whether the series has two items or five, whether its elements are words or phrases, it will break down into base sentences having parallel structures and repeated parts. If you have followed a consistent pattern in your deletions, your surface series will reflect clear parallelism. If you were inconsistent, checking the base sentences will help clear up your trouble.

With this trick, you should have an easy time maintaining parallelism among the units of a series joined by coordinating conjunctions. Correlative conjunctions, though, can be a bit confusing. Faced with an *either . . . or* situation, many writers go astray. The rule on parallelism requires that whatever type of grammatical unit follows the first of the conjunctive pair must also follow the second. To see how this works, we can take a simple-minded example. Your friends have stepped out for an evening of culture, but you're not sure where they were going. You could say,

> *Either they went to the opera*
> *   or they went to the concert,*

with a full clause following *either* and *or.* You could say,

> *They either went to the opera*
> *   or went to the concert,*

with *they* deleted in the second base sentence and a complete predicate following each correlative. You could say,

> *They went either to the opera*
> *   or to the concert,*

with *they went* deleted and a prepositional phrase following each of the conjunctions. Finally, you could say,

> *They went to either the opera*
> *   or the concert,*

with *they went to* deleted and a noun prepositional object following each conjunction. But you shouldn't say (or, at least, shouldn't <u>write</u>),

> *Either they went to the opera*
> *or   to the concert*

or

> *They either went to the opera*
> *or   the concert*

or any other version in which dissimilar units follow the two parts of the correlative conjunction—bad parallelism.

There is no requirement that you have to delete repeated elements. You may delete as much or as little of a repeated group of words as you wish, or you may choose to delete nothing. Bear one point in mind, though. Every time you delete a word needed in the grammar of its base sentence, you are forcing your reader to reconstruct it, subconsciously or consciously. Reconstruction is usually so automatic that a reader is unaware of having filled in the missing pieces. But if deletion goes too far, the reader may find it difficult to supply the missing words accurately. When this happens, the reader has to guess how the words relate to each other. Even a tiny "unnecessary" word like a repeated preposition should not always be deleted, because it can act as a useful guide to your reader. Repetition is irksome in a sentence like this: *The recipe calls for a mixture of butter, of sugar, of eggs, of milk, and of flour.* But in the next sentence, the repeated *with* sorts out the word groups and prevents misreading: *Elizabethan printers and publishers were hedged about with official restrictions on the book trade and with the internal regulations of the Stationers' Company, to which most bookmen belonged.* Don't delete to the point of confusion. Consider your reader.

The term *parallelism* extends beyond units within a single clause to describe the repetition of larger grammatical elements, used as an organizational device. When parallelism appears within a clause, the key concept is deletion. When parallelism appears <u>between</u> clauses, the key concept is repetition. As these last two sentences illustrate, you can repeat structures and whole clumps of words, changing only the significant words that create (in this case) contrast. Parallel structures clarify enumeration (*First, you take the . . . . Next, you add the . . . . Finally, you put the . . .*). It is an effective method for stressing the relation between ideas so that your readers can follow your chain of thought.

Parallel structures, moreover, can provide a powerful tool for hammering home important messages. Think how much more emphatic is the insistently repetitive *government of the people, by the people, for the people* than the simpler and flatter *government of, by, and for the people. Give me liberty or death* lacks the ringing echo of *Give me liberty or give me death.* Parallelism of this sort is a matter not of grammar but of stylistic manipulation to achieve a desired effect on the audience. Masterfully used, parallelism beats on our pulses, as Churchill demonstrated in his stirring speech to the House of Commons in the black summer of 1940:

> We shall not flag or fail. We shall fight in France, we shall fight on the seas and oceans, we shall fight with growing confidence and growing strength in the air, we shall defend our island, whatever the cost may be, we shall fight on the beaches, we shall fight on the landing grounds, we shall fight in the fields and in the streets, we shall fight in the hills; we shall never surrender.

28

Forms Seen
But Not Heard

You are no doubt familiar with the idea that you have at least three overlapping stocks of words: an active stock that you use daily in speech, a larger and less active stock that you draw upon when you write, and a still larger and somewhat passive stock that you recognize when you read. Your writing and reading vocabularies contain words you would seldom speak, and probably a few you can't even pronounce.

You also have several stocks of syntax. There are many grammatical forms that seem to live only, or at least mainly, in writing. Not even lawyers talk like a typical government regulation. Some sentences are peculiar to written English merely because of their length and complexity, although their component parts—adverbial clauses, prepositional phrases—are common enough. But other sentences have structural oddities and stylistic characteristics fairly specific to written grammar.

The subjunctive mood is an instance of a moribund form living more in print than in speech. It is still heard in statements obviously contrary to fact: *If I were running this firm, I'd give everyone a bonus.* It is somewhat more frequently seen in writing: *If it were not for electricity, modern life would resemble that of the Victorian Age.* This sentence could take a

136

further twist: *Were it not for electricity, modern life would resemble that of the Victorian Age.* Notice the deleted subordinating conjunction *if*—one more case in which a surface-structure dependent clause lacks its head word. Notice also the inverted verb–subject word order, required because of the deleted *if.*

Inversions also regularly occur in negated clauses; that is, clauses opening with a negative word. Sometimes a negative appears at the head of a sentence for emphasis: *Never had Johnstown seen such a flood.* Sometimes the negative is a conjunction joining two clauses: *It could not fly, nor could it float.* In either case, the subject of the negated clause has to move behind the auxiliary of its verb phrase.

The correlative pair *not only . . . but also* demonstrates this quirk. Used within a clause, the pair needs the usual parallel structures following each member, so that you might have *The compound is not only insoluble but also amorphous,* with parallel adjectives, but not **The compound is not only insoluble, but it is also amorphous,* an incorrect adjective+clause coupling. If the correlatives each <u>head</u> a clause, however, you no longer use parallel structure, for the first clause is negated and so must be inverted: *Not only is the compound insoluble, but it is also amorphous.* Rules supersede rules.

These negatives inversions are required. Another kind of inversion is optional, a stylistic choice for emphasis or dramatic effect, as in, *Compromise he totally abhorred.* Here it is the object that has been switched, moving from its usual post-verb spot to the head of the sentence. Sometimes it is predicate adjectives that are pulled forward: *Calm and prosperous though the nation appeared, inwardly it seethed with discontent.*

The openings of written sentences often receive unusual stylistic treatments. Perhaps an appositive heads the sentence: *Money, power, fame—these were the goals of his life.* Perhaps the sentence begins with a string of repeated parallel structures: *When the firing ceased, when the troops withdrew, when the wounded were treated and the dead removed, when dusk finally shaded the bloody field, only then did the general realize the extent of his losses.* Notice, again, the required inversion in the final clause.

Sometimes it is the end of a sentence that gets the extended repetitions: *The stock market continued its dizzy plunge, ruining brokers, wiping out large speculators, impoverishing small investors, closing banks, shutting down factories, choking trade, dragging whole nations in its destructive wake.*

You may have observed that this last example contains a series of items separated by commas but lacking a final conjunction. The omission of a normal *and* gives an open-ended effect to the series: it suggests that you could give still further instances of the market's devastation and are inviting your reader to add to the list. An opposite technique is to omit all commas, placing *and* before each series item: *The crash ruined brokers and large speculators and small investors and banks and factories and trade and whole nations.* Here the effect is one of cumulative force, as item after item after item is tacked onto the sentence, with again an invitation to continue.

Another device obvious only in writing (though sometimes heard in slightly incoherent speech) is the insertion of a totally separate and complete sentence within another sentence: *The summer of 1967 (how well we remember!) brought new shocks to the country.* These parenthetical sentences can be punctuated, when appropriate, with exclamation points or question marks, but never with periods: *Whether or not Benedict Arnold intended treason (the question has never been fully resolved), he bore a traitor's infamy.*

There is no point in continuing this brief catalogue of unusual forms in written syntax, because variety in sentences is limited only by the ingenuity of writers. Many of the forms shown here have a distinctly literary flavor, more at home in fiction than in factual prose. Yet, if not overdone and if carefully chosen to produce a specific desired effect, they can be useful in any kind of writing.

Sentences come in all sorts of sizes and shapes. You should aim for an interesting mix. You need a good many ordinary, comfortable, workaday sentences, neither too long and complex, nor too short and stark. But once in a while a short sentence adds zing and a lengthy sentence adds weight. Occasionally you will even want the flourish of a well-crafted showpiece. It feels good to flex your syntactic muscles. And it also wakes up your readers.

29

Some Tips
on Style

We have strayed a bit far afield from grammar and encroached upon the area of style. Style itself is a rather vague, ill-defined quality of writing. Although not every literary expert would agree, we have been using the word *style* to cover all those options and choices that writers face in deciding how best to present their ideas. Grammar is relatively rigid: if you write an adverbial clause, you must construct it to meet certain criteria. But you may <u>choose</u> to place that clause at the beginning or at the end of your sentence. Or you may <u>choose</u> not to use the full clause at all, but to reduce it to an adverbial prepositional phrase. So there are stylistic options even within the confines of grammar.

Style, of course, extends to far larger problems in writing: your approach to your subject, your attitude toward your audience, the tone and level of formality you desire, the number of examples or depth of explanation you feel is needed for an effective presentation of your ideas. These and other considerations, all vitally important to the act of writing, go past the bounds of this book. Here we are not concerned with how to write. We are concerned with how to use written grammar.

Certain points of style, however, do impinge directly

enough upon grammar to merit our attention. One such grammar-style question involves the length of sentences.

There is no "ideal" sentence length, either stylistically or grammatically. So far as grammar goes, there is not even a theoretic limit to the length of a sentence. If food is good, it can be very good, or very very good, or very very very good, *ad infinitum.* Or we could make endless "Jack-built" sentences: *This is the cow that kicked the dog that chased the cat that killed the rat that ate the malt that lay in the house that Jack built.* So much for grammar, then. Sentences can grow indefinitely.

Stylistically, however, there are a few considerations, if no actual limits. For one thing, you should be able to read a sentence aloud without gasping for breath. Periods provide obvious breathing spots, but commas can also give you a chance for air. So observe the breath test: punctuate or terminate your sentences to allow for your readers' lungs. As a second consideration, keep your readers' ease of comprehension in mind. A sentence should not be so long or so complex that your readers forget how it started. If you have too many phrases, clauses, and parenthetical comments within one sentence, then, even though they may all be grammatically linked up and masterfully punctuated, as the various elements in this sentence are, your readers might get lost—just as you perhaps got lost reading this rambler. For your readers' sake, break up unusually long or complicated sentences into more easily digestible portions.

A second grammar-style tip: It's quite all right to begin a sentence with *and* or *but* or some other coordinating conjunction, just as it is all right to end a sentence with a particle or a preposition. Most people remember stern injunctions against both these practices from their early schooling. But grammatically, there is no rule against either. Stylistically, an opening conjunction or a closing preposition might be weak. Or it might be highly effective. So follow your instincts, not the ghostly voice of some misguided teacher who didn't know what writing is all about.

Next point: Repetition, either of individual words or of larger parallel structures, is emphatic and effective when used correctly, because it draws attention to the repeated elements. For the same reason, it is distracting or boring when used carelessly—distracting because the reader first tries to figure out why his attention is being solicited, boring after the reader realizes that the only noteworthy point is the writer's limited vocabulary and syntax. That kind of attention you don't need. Therefore, deliberately repeat a key word or structure when you want to emphasize it. If you are discussing voting rights, repeat *voting rights* as often as necessary. Don't strain for variety with confusing or amusing synonyms like *franchise, suffrage, ballot privileges, show of hands,* and *nose-counts.* On the other hand, if you don't wish to stress a word or structure, avoid needless and meaningless repetitions. Even repeated sounds can be annoying. To comb out unintentional repetitions, rhymes, and chingalings, read your writing aloud and listen to the sounds of the words. You may be surprised!

Another tip: Don't try to "correct" an awkward or weak sentence. If you notice an actual error in your writing—say, non-agreement between a subject and its verb—you can easily rectify that. But if the sentence seems formless or confusing, don't think you can cure it by changing a word or patching in a comma. Toss the whole thing out and start again. You keep the idea that you wish to convey, but you recast the idea into some better structure. Even a grammatically proper sentence sometimes sounds illiterate, like *Neither he nor I am ready.* It's correct, but toss it out, too. You should be aware by now of the many varieties of ways you have to "say the same thing." So just keep trying a different way, until you come up with a form that carries your meaning effectively, clearly, rhythmically, precisely, and pleasingly.

The next thing to remember is that in a conflict between style and grammar, style usually wins, and properly so. Grammar rules describe the normal, the expected. For the most part, you should try to write normally and acceptably. But if you need the unexpected for special effect—a forceful jolt to your readers, a sudden twist—break the usual patterns. The "mistake" will call attention to the point you wish to emphasize; if it is deliberate and effective, it's not a mistake at all. The four essential rules of grammar that we met earlier and the three others that appear in the next section <u>are</u> relatively sacrosanct. You needn't always choose, though, to write a full grammatical sentence (rule #1), and normal word order (rule #2) is frequently transposed. Bending the rule on coordination and parallelism can supply intentional humor: *He got out of his wet clothes and into a dry martini,* to cite Alexander Woollcott's famous *mot.* The moral: if you know normal, correct grammar, you can then manipulate words and punctuation as you will, for your own stylistic purposes. You need no longer slavishly follow the advice of books and teachers. <u>You</u> become the master.

The final bit of grammar-style advice is one you have heard over and over again in this book: Trust your instincts. Never underestimate the value of your ear. <u>Speak</u> your writing and listen for undesirable repetitions and ambiguous constructions. Use the breath test to judge your sentence lengths and the voice-contour test to check your punctuation. Good grammar sounds good. Good writing is speakable. And who wants unsound grammar or unspeakable writing?

VII

Sampling the Nitty-Gritty

30

Verbs
and Verb Phrases

Although by this time you have learned quite a bit about English verbs, you still haven't been given an organized breakdown of the forms for verbs and verb phrases. The forms are rather numerous and more than a bit complex. They are also quite precise. You can't be "sort of close" in your verb formation: you either have it or you don't. This chapter illustrates the finer points of verb forms, one of the rigorous areas in the nitty-gritty of grammar, where *right* and *wrong* are operative words. Some of the material you've met before, but it's repeated here just to collect all the facts on verb forms into one handy reference chapter.

PRINCIPAL PARTS

We shall begin with the five so-called *principal parts* of verbs: the infinitive, the present and past tense forms, and the present and past participles. With some verbs, the principal parts have different forms; with other verbs, two or three of the principal parts may have the same form (that is, they are spelled the same). Here are the five principal parts, along with some example verbs:

1. Infinitive—the basic form of the verb as listed in a dictionary. Because it indicates no tense (time) limitations, it is infinite; hence, its name. When it appears in a sentence, an infinitive is often, but not always, preceded by the infinitive marker *to*.

(to) jump   (to) break   (to) hit   (to) have   (to) be

2. Present tense—usually resembles the form of the infinitive, but adds an *-s* in the third person singular.

jump(s)   break(s)   hit(s)   have, has   am, is, are

3. Past tense—formed by adding *-ed* to the infinitive, or by respelling the root of the verb, or by doing nothing. Referred to as the *-ed* form.

jumped   broke   hit   had   was, were

4. Present participle—formed by adding *-ing* to the infinitive (possibly involving a doubled final consonant or a dropped final *e*). Referred to as the *-ing* form.

jumping   breaking   hitting   having   being

5. Past participle—formed by adding *-en* to the verb, or by adding *-ed* (in which case it looks like the past tense), or by respelling the root of the verb, or by doing nothing. Referred to as the *-en* form.

jumped   broken   hit   had   been

SUMMARY OF PRINCIPAL PARTS.

<u>All</u> verbs end in *-s* in the third person singular present tense.

<u>All</u> verbs form the present participle by adding *-ing* to the infinitive form.

<u>Most</u> verbs are so-called "regular verbs," like *jump*. Both the past tense and the past participle of regular verbs are formed by adding *-ed*.

Irregular verbs show great variety in the ways they form the past tense and the past participle (such as *break, broke, broken; think, thought, thought; drink, drank, drunk*). Either memorize these irregular verbs or check their forms in a dictionary.

Infinitive	*jump*	*break*	*hit*	*have*	*be*
Present Tense	*jump*(s)	*break*(s)	*hit*(s)	*have, has*	*am, is, are*
Past Tense	*jumped*	*broke*	*hit*	*had*	*was, were*
Present Participle	*jumping*	*breaking*	*hitting*	*having*	*being*
Past Participle	*jumped*	*broken*	*hit*	*had*	*been*

MAIN VERBS

A grammatically complete sentence or any clause must have a finite verb, often called a **main verb**, in order to indicate the tense of the sentence or clause. The main verb may be either a simple verb or a verb phrase.

There are only two true tenses in English verbs: the **simple present** tense and the **simple past** tense.

> *The students study verbs.*   (simple present tense)
> *The students studied verbs.*   (simple past tense)

All other indications of tense (time) are shown by putting together verb phrases of varying lengths, such as these:

> *The students are studying verbs.*
> *The students will be studying verbs.*

*The students **should have been studying** verbs.*
*The students **ought to have studied** verbs in eighth grade.*

FORMS OF PRESENT TENSE AND PAST TENSE MAIN VERBS.

The **simple present tense** uses the same form as the infinitive in all persons, singular and plural, except for the third person singular, which adds an *-s.* Note the great irregularity of *be.*

Singular

1st person	*I walk*	*I have*	*I am*
2nd person	*you walk*	*you have*	*you are*
3rd person	*he walks*	*she has*	*it is*

Plural

1st person	*we walk*	*we have*	*we are*
2nd person	*you walk*	*you have*	*you are*
3rd person	*they walk*	*they have*	*they are*

The **simple past tense** (formed by adding *-ed* to regular-verb infinitives or by making the required changes in irregular verbs) uses the same form in all persons and numbers. The only exception is found in the verb *be.*

Singular

1st person	*I walked*	*I had*	*I was*
2nd person	*you walked*	*you had*	*you were*
3rd person	*he walked*	*she had*	*it was*

Plural

1st person	*we walked*	*we had*	*we were*
2nd person	*you walked*	*you had*	*you were*
3rd person	*they walked*	*they had*	*they were*

These two tenses are the only verb forms that can function <u>alone</u> as main verbs in sentences. All other main verbs are verb phrases consisting of verbals and auxiliaries.

VERBALS. Infinitives, present participles, and past participles are called *verbals* ("resembling a verb") because they are derived from verbs and act somewhat like verbs. That is, they sometimes have subjects and objects (either or both), and they may be modified by adverbs. But when used alone without auxiliaries, verbals function as nominals, adjectivals, or adverbials. A verbal <u>cannot</u> function alone as the main verb of a clause.

> *The man **to win** the election.*   (infinitive used as an adjectival)
>
> ***Swimming** in the river.*   (present participle used as a noun, sometimes known as a *gerund*)
>
> *The duck **swimming** in the river.*   (present participle used as an adjectival)
>
> *The reason **being** a lack of funds.*   (present participle used in an absolute)
>
> *The cup **broken** on the floor.*   (past participle used as an adjectival)

VERB PHRASES AS MAIN VERBS. Verbals can also be used as part of a verb phrase that functions as the main verb of a clause, but they must always have the proper kinds of auxiliary verbs preceding them. The first auxiliary in a verb phrase indicates the **tense** and sometimes the **mode**; the verbal indicates the idea or meaning of the verb phrase. The most commonly used auxiliary verbs are *be, have, will,* and *do.* Verb phrases follow certain definite patterns that must be observed. The pattern depends upon the particular verbal being used.

> 1. **The infinitive.**
>   A. The infinitive is used with the modal auxiliary verb *will* to indicate futurity.
>
>   *They **will** win.* (Note that the infinitive marker *to* is usually omitted in verb phrases.)
>
>   *He **will be** leaving tomorrow.*
>
>   *The play **will have** begun before we arrive.*

B. The infinitive is used with other modal auxiliaries (*can, could, must, may, might, shall, should, would, ought*) to indicate different shadings of modes, such as determination, possibility, or obligation.

*We **must work** hard.*

*You **may be** wasting your money.*

*John **ought** to **have won**.*

C. The infinitive is used with a form of the auxiliary verb *do* to make an emphatic assertion, to make a negative statement, or to ask a question.

*Grammar **does make** sense at times.* (emphasis)

*Dogs **do** not **like** cats.* (negation)

***Did** the book **end** happily?* (question)

2. *The present participle.*
The present participle is used to indicate continuing action. It must always be preceded by some form of the auxiliary verb *be*.
Verb phrase form: ***be*** + (verb)-*ing*

*Tommy **is eating**.*

*Mary **was being** stubborn.*

*They had **been racing***

*He will **be leaving** tomorrow.*

3. *The past participle.*
A. In the **active voice**, the past participle must always be preceded by some form of the auxiliary verb *have*.
Verb phrase form (active voice): **have** + (verb)-**en**

*Tommy **has eaten**.*

*Tommy **had eaten**.*

*They **had been** racing.*

*The play will **have begun**.*

B. In the **passive voice**, the past participle must always be preceded by some form of the auxiliary verb *be*.†
Verb phrase form (passive voice): **be** + (verb)**-en**

*Tommy **is eaten** by the purple people eater.*

*The paper **was delivered** by the paper boy.*

*The money might have **been stolen.***

*The initiative will have **to be taken** quickly.*

SUMMARY OF VERB PHRASES. Tense is always shown by the auxiliary part of the verb phrase; meaning, by the verbal part; shadings of meaning, by modal auxiliaries.

	Auxiliary		*Verbal*
Active Voice	**will**	+	**infinitive**
	modal	+	**infinitive**
	do	+	**infinitive**
	be	+	**(verb)-ing**
	have	+	**(verb)-en**
Passive Voice	**be**	+	**(verb)-en**

ORDER OF AUXILIARY VERBS. When a verb phrase consists of several auxiliaries before the verbal, the following order is always observed:

	(1) modal	+ (2) *have*	+ (3) *be*	+ (4) verbal
He	*could*	*have*	*been*	*killed.*
It	*might*		*be*	*forgotten.*
It		*has*	*been*	*forgotten.*

†Despite the "always" in this statement, passive sentences sometimes have *get* as the auxiliary verb: *The shipment got damaged in transit.* The same "*get* + past participle" phrase appears in expressions like *Don't get lost* or *It's time to get started.* And *get* can also be used in active sentences with the present participle of certain verbs: *She got going on her project.* These *get* usages occur mostly in idioms or in casual, conversational writing. They also prove what you should realize by now, that grammar precepts containing *always* or *never* require several grains of salt.

She	should	have		finished.	
They	will		be	sleeping.	
He	would	have	been	driving.	
She	must	have		had	fun.

Note the parts of the verb phrase *could have been killed*. *Killed* is a past participle, used with a form of *be* to make the passive voice. The form of *be* here is *been*, the past participle used with a form of *have*. *Have* in this phrase is the infinitive form, used with the modal auxiliary *could*. These, then, are the four pieces of the phrase. As to the message they communicate, *killed* carries the basic idea of the verb phrase, but the idea is modulated by the auxiliaries. *Been killed* indicates the voice of the verb phrase (here, passive). *Could have been* indicates the tense and the mode of the verb phrase; that is, the action referred to would have occurred some time in the past, except that it didn't really happen, although there was a possibility of its happening—all that meaning in three little auxiliary verbs!

POSTSCRIPT

All of the verb forms discussed in this chapter have been in the **indicative** mood: they indicate or make a statement about something. Verbs may also appear in the **imperative** and the **subjunctive** moods.

The imperative verb form is identical to the infinitive form: *Stop! Please sit down.* The imperative form is used to give a direct or an implied command.

The subjunctive verb form is rather rapidly dying out in English usage. It still appears in carefully worded statements that are contrary to fact, especially in the expression *if I were you.* It also is found in a few other traditional places, such as *Please be seated* or *They insisted that the chairman resign.* If you are really curious about the forms and uses of the subjunctive, consult a detailed book on English grammar.

31

Agreement

Verbs are the only English words that change forms to show *tense* (*birds fly* vs. *birds flew*). They also change forms to show different *numbers* (*it runs* vs. *they run*). So do nouns (*book* vs. *books*) and pronouns (*I* vs. *we*). And verbs change forms to show different *persons* (*you eat* vs. *he eats*). So do pronouns (*you* vs. *he*). Pronouns change forms to show three different *cases* (*they, them,* and *their*); nouns show only two (*dog* and *dog's*). Finally, only pronouns have different forms for different *genders* (*he, she,* and *it*). These special forms for number, person, case, and gender are all interrelated in an intricate network of **agreement** within a sentence, a network that—to mix metaphors—is pockmarked with loopholes and pitfalls. Let us investigate.

Agreement is one grammatical term that means exactly what it says. When a verb *agrees* with its subject, both subject and verb must be, say, singular. Or when a pronoun *agrees* with the noun it replaces, both must be, say, feminine. Basically, agreement is dictated by grammar. But sometimes usage—the language practices of respected speakers of English—overrules strict grammatical precepts. We shall not be looking at all the rules and exceptions in this cloudy area. You'll get a general survey of agreement, though, with enough odd situations to alert you to the need for caution. Handbooks on grammar and usage can fill in the thornier details.

We shall start with the concept of **number**. English uses only two numbers, *singular* and *plural*. The rule concerning number seems straightforward enough: A subject and its verb must agree in number. Hence the shifting *-s* in these two sentences:

> *The boy plays baseball.*
> *The boys play baseball.*

Suppose those boys form a baseball team. Would you say *The team play* or *The team plays*? Because the word *team* represents a group of people, it is called a *collective noun*. Other collective nouns include *jury, family, class* (of students), and *board* (of governors). Although a collective noun refers to more than one individual, it takes a singular verb if the individuals are treated collectively as a group: ***The jury has reached its verdict.*** But the same collective noun would take a plural verb if its members are considered as individuals: ***The jury have reached conflicting verdicts.*** Though this latter sentence is correct, it sounds wrong. The best advice is to use a singular verb with a collective noun, considering the noun always as a group. If you wish to discuss individuals within the group, just change the wording: ***The jury members have reached conflicting verdicts.***

A second problem in subject–verb agreement arises when a dummy subject, or expletive, starts the sentence, postponing the true subject to a spot behind the verb. With the dummy subject *there,* the verb is either singular or plural, depending on the number of the true subject: ***There is a fly in the ointment*** or ***There are three flies in the ointment.*** But with the dummy subject *it,* the verb is always singular: ***It was two weeks before the news reached London.***

A third area of possible confusion develops when modifiers like *some, some of the, several of the, a few,* and *almost all* precede the headnoun subject. The whole noun phrase would be plural, and so would its verb: *Some of our aircraft are missing.* But when the phrase *none of the* modifies a subject noun, the noun phrase takes either a singular or a plural verb, depending on its meaning: ***None of the students has** a book,* or ***None of the men have drilled** together as a platoon.* Also, when the count phrase *one of the* or *not one of the* precedes the subject, the verb is always singular.

All of the sentence subjects we have discussed so far have been nouns or noun phrases. Pronouns functioning as subjects follow the same rule: singular pronoun, singular verb; plural pronoun, plural verb. Pronouns, though, have a few little quirks of their own. Quirk one: The pronoun *none* used as a subject takes either a singular or a plural verb, depending on the meaning of the sentence: *They needed one good man, but **none was** available,* or *They needed qualified electricians, but **none were** available.* You might compare this with the usage of *none of the,* shown above. Quirk two: The pronouns *everyone, everybody, everything, anyone, anybody, anything, someone, somebody, something,* and *no one, nobody, nothing*—all these pronouns, when used as subjects, require singular verbs: *Nobody was there. Everybody was there.* Whatever the nose count, the verb is singular.

We can look at one more number problem before pushing on. When the subject is an "either this or that" or a "neither this nor that" kind of correlative construction, and when "this" is singular and "that" is plural, what do you do with the verb? Simple. The verb agrees with the nearer of the two subject nouns. Hence, both of these sentences are correct:

Neither the students nor the teacher was in class.
Neither the teacher nor the students were in class.

And if you don't like either of those, try this:

The students weren't in class, and neither was the teacher.

The concept of **person** offers hardly any difficulties. English has three persons. The *first person* is the person doing the speaking. The *second person* is the person being spoken to. And the *third person* is the person or thing being spoken about. This is most clearly demonstrated in pronouns: *I* (the first-person speaker) say something to *you* (the second-person addressee) about *him* (the third-person topic of our gossip). All nouns are treated as being in the third person—things being talked about. The one exception is the so-called "noun of direct address": *Jim, I love you.* Here Jim is being spoken to, so the noun *Jim* is in the second person.

Verbs also show different forms for different persons, although only in a few selected spots. All present tense, third person, singular verbs end in -*s;* and the verb *to be* also shows additional person differences in both the present and the past tense. Otherwise, verb forms don't change for person, but only for tense and (sometimes) number.

The agreement rule governing person is again straightforward: A subject (especially a pronoun) and its verb must agree in person. Thus, *you read* but *he reads,* or *I was* but *you were.* Unfortunately, *to be,* the most irregular verb, turns up in countless verb phrases, so the need to be aware of person arises more frequently than you might assume. But the rule is simple; there are no exceptions; and you should have little trouble matching your persons in subject and verb.

We have now examined two aspects of subject–verb agreement and noted some of the problems that can arise from them. These problems are often tricky, but you must solve them in some fashion, because the agreement between a subject and its verb is an inviolable requirement in an English sentence. In fact, it underlies another essential rule of grammar, a rule that combines both number and person: **The subject (noun or pronoun) and its verb must agree in number and in person.**

We turn next to **gender.** What used to be an easy distinction between masculine, feminine, neuter, and generic has recently become a touchy sore spot full of emotional, social, and political controversy. Let's look at the easy distinctions first. Third-person singular pronouns use different forms for different genders: *he, him,* and *his* refer to *masculine* nouns; *she, her,* and *hers,* to *feminine* nouns; and *it* and *its,* to *neuter* nouns. So far, so good. Finally, there is a *generic* pronoun that refers indiscriminately to any human being, male or female. The traditional generic pronoun in English is *he* (*him, his*), which unluckily has the same form as the masculine pronoun. And here's where the fireworks ignite.

Since the generic *he* has no reference to sex, it is found in many expressions that apply to the whole human race. Take the proverb *He who hesitates is lost.* This saying is as true for women as for men. Yet some women today would object to it as discriminatorily sexist. Actually, it is both grammatically and semantically correct. However, if you strongly dislike the generic *he,* replace it with *he or she* and not with the unpronounceable *he/she.*

The generic pronoun also causes hard feelings in sentences using *everybody* or *everyone.* We saw that *everybody* takes a singular verb: *Everybody **was** there.* Although you might argue that *everybody* suggests a lot of people, no one says or writes **Everybody **were** there.* But if a subsequent pronoun refers to *everybody,* most of us tend to pluralize that pronoun. That is, we say *Everybody has **their** money.* This "error" is so common that it has become accepted usage in many speaking situations. But not in <u>writing</u> situations. When we write, we must still use a singular possessive: *Everybody has **his** money.* And there is that scratchy generic pronoun again—correct but (in some quarters) unpopular.

How can you handle it? In a sentence like *Everyone has*

his own special needs, the generic *his* is, to many readers, the one right form; so you can stand by your guns and use it. *His or her* is awkward, but you can go with it if you insist: *Everyone has his or her own special needs.* Sometimes you can fudge by pluralizing the subject: *All people have their own special needs.* Context, however, does not always permit this escape hatch. As a final measure, you might accept the guidance of the National Council of Teachers of English. In a resolution deploring sexism in language, the Council advocates your writing, "in all but strictly formal usage," the plural possessive in situations like this: *Everyone has their own special needs.* If you follow this advice, however, be prepared for a fight: to most educated readers, including many teachers of English, this written usage constitutes a flat grammatical error.

We have seen that subject pronouns must agree in number and person with their verbs. But pronouns usually represent nouns, and they must also agree with those nouns. The noun that a pronoun replaces is called either its **antecedent** (because the noun usually falls into the writing before the pronoun) or its **referent** (because the noun is what the pronoun refers to). *Referent* is the more logical term, but *antecedent* seems to be the more common. So we shall use *antecedent.* In the sentence *When the president breakfasted with the senators, he thanked them for their cooperation,* the antecedent of *he* is *the president* and the antecedent of *them* and *their* is *the senators.* Both antecedents are in the third person, and so are all the pronouns. *The president* is singular and masculine, and so is *he. The senators* is plural, and so are *them* and *their* (gender gets lost in plurality). The sentence, then, demonstrates our next agreement rule, which also happens to be one of the "musts" of grammar: **A pronoun and its antecedent must agree in gender, number, and person.**

Finally, we must look at the concept of grammatical case. **Case** refers to form changes in nouns and pronouns to reflect different functions within a clause. Nouns have only one case change: when a noun indicates possession, it adds an "apostrophe -s." This change varies somewhat for plural nouns or for nouns already ending in *s*. For these niceties, consult a usage handbook. But the principle is quite ordinary: *the bird's nest; the girl's dress.* Otherwise, nouns have no case endings.

Personal pronouns (*I, you, he, she, it, we,* and *they*) have three case forms—subjective, objective, and possessive. The *subjective* form is used when the pronoun functions as the subject of a verb (*They shall inherit the earth*) or as the complement of a linking verb (*It was he*). The *objective* form is used when the pronoun functions as the object of a verb (*Let them eat cake*) or the object of a preposition (*The house was designed for her*). The *possessive* form is used when the pronoun "owns" the noun it modifies (*The elephant raised its trunk*). Note that the possessive form of *it* is *its,* with no apostrophe, just as there is no apostrophe in *his, hers, ours,* and *yours.* With an apostrophe, *it's* is the contraction of *it is.*

The relative pronoun *who* also has three distinct case forms: *who, whom,* and *whose.* But the other two relative pronouns, *which* and *that,* have the same form for the subjective and objective cases and lack a possessive case. *Who* and *whom* refer to persons, *which* refers to things, and *that* refers restrictively to either persons or things. The possessive form *whose* can also refer to either persons or things. One hundred years ago you would have had to write, *Discard any book the pages of which are torn.* That's still acceptable, but today the simpler version is preferred: *Discard any book whose pages are torn.*

All of these examples serve to illustrate our final agreement rule and our final "must": **The case of a pronoun must agree with the function of the pronoun within its clause or phrase.** Occasionally, this rule gets involved in some trick sentences, like this somewhat similar pair:

> *Vote for the man whom you prefer.*
> *Vote for the man who you think is best.*

In both sentences the relative pronouns (*whom* and *who*) relate their adjectival clauses to the same antecedent, *man.* But within the two adjectival (or relative) clauses, the pronouns function differently. *Whom* is the object of the verb *prefer* (*you prefer whom*), so it must be in the objective case. On the other hand, *who* functions as the subject of the verb *is* (*who is best*), so it must be in the subjective case. Sometimes the correct versions sound strange. You may recall an earlier sample noun-clause sentence, *Give help to whoever needs it.* Since *whoever* is the subject of *needs,* it requires the subjective case. (The object of the preposition *to* is the whole noun clause.) If that sentence jars on your ear, you don't need to write it. Instead say, *Whoever needs help should get it.* When two ways are right, pick the way that sounds better.

You met four essential "musts" of English back in Chapter 8 and were promised three more. Scattered through this chapter are those additional rules. Let's bring them all together for one final quick review.

1. *A grammatical sentence must have at least one independent clause.*

2. *The normal word order of a clause is*
   SUBJECT + PREDICATE
                    ⎣———→ *VERB (+ optional elements).*

3. *The main verb of a clause must be finite in form.*

4. *The subject (noun or pronoun) and its verb must agree in number and in person.*

5. *A pronoun and its antecedent must agree in gender, in number, and in person.*

6. *The case of a pronoun must agree with the function of the pronoun within its clause or phrase.*

7. *Coordinating and correlative conjunctions must join equal grammatical units.*

There you have them—the seven absolute rules of written English grammar. All else in writing is a matter of judgment, of deliberate choice, of stylistic options. When you face a situation involving one of these seven rules, ask yourself the easy question—"What is right?" When you face any other writing problem, ask yourself the harder but more stimulating question—"What is best?"

32

Mechanical
Punctuation

The punctuation devices that we examined earlier are closely allied to grammatical structures and to the contours and stresses of the spoken words. There is a second, far less interesting, kind of punctuation—the arbitrary conventions that always appear in certain situations. These are marks such as the colon in times, like *2:45 P.M.*, and the periods after abbreviations, like *c.o.d.* and *N.Y.* These conventions are important, but they belong in a book on mechanics, not a book on grammar.

You need to be familiar with the forms used in your particular profession or office, for mechanics often follow idiosyncratic "house rules." The military, for instance, write *1445* instead of *2:45 P.M.* And certain abbreviations, such as *NASA* and *NATO*, are customarily written without periods. So check the approved forms for your area of expertise.

Two problems in mechanical punctuation are worth a brief mention here, though—the first because students always ask about it, the second because they seldom are even aware that a problem exists.

The question that always comes up involves the combination of quotation marks with other punctuation. Do commas and periods go inside the closing quotation mark, or outside?

The quick answer is, they go inside, always. But if you know <u>why</u> they go inside, you may have an easier time remembering the rule. Don't try to reason out the proper position, for the answer derives not from logic, but from aesthetics!

Consider this sentence:

In the poem "Invictus," Henley strikes an agnostic note.

The comma after *Invictus* is logically not part of the title of the poem. Why, then, is it inside the quotation marks? Because it is

prettier. American printers have decided that ". and ",

look awkward, unbalanced. But ." and ," have eye appeal, a better artistic composition. Hence the rule. Larger marks of punctuation—semicolons, colons, question marks, and exclamation points—are sturdy enough to balance themselves, so that

you write either "? or ?" depending upon the logic of the quotation or of the whole sentence within which the quotation appears. (Logically, colons and semicolons almost never precede a closing quotation mark.) The tiny marks, however, the little periods and commas, have to be tucked inside the protective final quotation mark for appearance's sake. British printers, incidentally, ignore this artistic nicety: they put all marks either inside or outside the final quotation mark, according to the logic of the particular sentence. We, though, are Americans, so we enclose our small marks.

The question that seldom arises concerns the use (more frequently, the abuse) of hyphens. Few persons realize that hyphens follow rules. Let's begin with a simple rule: to type a hyphen, hit letterhyphenletter, with no intervening spaces. To type a dash, hit letterhyphenhyphenletter, again with no spaces. Now let's see how hyphens work.

Hyphens are used in compound words, such as *manic-*

depressive and *secretary-treasurer.* "Self" words are always hyphenated: *self-taught, self-conscious, self-starter,* and similar compounds. Never trust your memory on the spelling of compounds. What used to be *co-star* ten years ago is today *costar.* To be safe, check suspected compound words in a current dictionary, for styles in hyphenation change fairly rapidly.

Hyphens are often used in compound modifiers that precede their nouns, as *a **well-built** car* or *a **clear-cut** decision.* But if those same compound modifiers appear after a linking verb, the hyphen is omitted: *The car is **well built**. The decision was **clear cut**.* The hyphen serves to prevent misreading by clearly telling the reader which words go with which. Suppose you wrote the phrase *a stock racing car.* Your reader would not know whether the car is used in stock racing or whether the racing car is a stock model. With a hyphen, *a stock-racing car,* the doubt cannot arise. Where there can be no chance of misreading, you don't need the hyphen: *a more exciting movie, the atomic energy program.* If these compound modifiers fall after a linking verb, there is seldom a possibility of confusion and hence seldom a need for the hyphen. Don't overhyphenate your compound modifiers, but do use a hyphen any time it increases clarity.

Finally and most importantly, a hyphen is used to split a word at the end of a line. Several rules limit how and where you can split a word. For example, the split must be between pronounced syllables, which means that a one-syllable word can't be divided, no matter how long it is. Don't split off one letter at the front of a word, like *a-bove.* (Wrong!) Don't split off two letters at the end, like *tested.* (Wrong!) Split between prefixes and word stems, as *trans-port* and not *tran-sport.* (Wrong!) Don't split so that the first group of letters forms an unrelated word that gives your readers a false expectation of what follows on the next line, especially when the "odd" word also has a different pronunciation, like *comedies.* (Wrong!) Last of all, hyphenate hyphenated words only at the hyphen. This sounds like double-talk, but it means merely that a word containing its own hyphen, like *self-confident,* should be hyphenated only as *self-confident* and never as *self-con-fident* (wrong!) or *self-confi-dent* (wrong!). You'll find a few other rules on word division in mechanics handbooks, but these are the main ones. The point is that you don't hyphenate a word just because you've run out of space at the end of a line. You have to observe the rules. And you have to know there <u>are</u> rules.

33

A Few Pointers on Spelling

Spelling, like quotation marks and hyphens, is really a mechanical aspect of writing. This book is not the place for a lengthy discussion of spelling rules and exceptions. Grammar, however, involves word forms; these forms involve certain grammatical suffixes; and attaching these suffixes involves changes in spelling. So it seems appropriate to point out a few of the spelling problems that can arise in grammar. (If you have no spelling problems, you have no need to read this chapter.)

In plural nouns and in third person, singular, present tense verbs an -s must often be attached to the base word. Several situations require additional spelling changes before the -s can be attached. If the base word ends in any kind of sibilant, like s or sh or ch, an e must be inserted to give the suffix -s a separate syllable sound. Hence, *glass, glasses; rush, rushes; fetch, fetches.* If the base word ends in o, an e is again usually inserted: *tomato, tomatoes; go, goes.* If the base word ends in a y, two possible situations arise, each with its own rule. When the y is preceded by a consonant, the y is changed to i and an e is inserted before the suffix -s: *lady, ladies; rely, relies.* But if a vowel precedes the y, there is no change. Only the suffix -s is attached: *boy, boys, buy, buys.* So much for -s.

The same "y" rules apply when you add *-er* or *-est* to adjectives and adverbs ending in *y*. With a preceding consonant, change *y* to *i*: *silly, sillier, silliest*. With a preceding vowel, no change: *gray, grayer, grayest*.

With verbs, two more suffixes concern us: the *-ed* appearing on many past tense and past participle forms, and the *-ing* signaling a present participle. When *-ed* is attached to a verb ending in *y*, you again follow the "y" rules that you've already met. With a consonant preceding the *y*, you change *y* to *i* and add *-ed*: *defy, defied*. But with a vowel preceding it, you merely add *-ed*: *convey, conveyed*. The *y* is <u>never</u> changed when *-ing* is added, because changing the *y* to *i* would produce the very un-English look of two consecutive *i*'s. So you write both *defying* and *conveying*.

The next peculiarity involves verbs whose final (or only) syllable has either a short or a long accented vowel. The difference between short and long vowels can be seen in the following word pairs (with the short vowel first in each pair):

cap	*cape*
met	*mete*
shin	*shine*
cop	*cope*
tub	*tube*

At this point, we are going to meet some symbols: V for *vowel* and C for *consonant*. If you don't care for algebra, you may find the rest of this discussion a shade confusing. On the other hand, you may discover that spelling suddenly makes sense. If the following explanations help you, fine. But if they cause your head to spin, don't worry about the next three paragraphs. All of these spelling tips are offered in the hope that they may perhaps prove enlightening. What brings light to some persons, though, brings darkness to others. Luckily, there's nothing compulsory about understanding these explanations—or even reading them.

Back to the short and long vowels. Notice that each "short vowel" word ends in a single consonant directly following the short vowel. That is, it has a vowel–consonant combination or, using our symbols, a V–C sequence. In each "long vowel" word, however, the long vowel precedes a consonant and another vowel. Using our shorthand again, each "long vowel" word has a V–C–V sequence. This V–C–V sequence is what causes the first vowel in the sequence to be long. The second vowel in each of the words in our list is the so-called "silent *e*."

Now, when *-ed* is added to a "long vowel" verb that ends in a silent *e* (like *cope*, V–C–V), one of the *e*'s disappears. We might as well say that the verb drops the silent *e* and adds *-ed*. When *-ing* is added, again the verb drops its silent *e*. The result in each case is a new V–C–V sequence (*coped* and *coping*), and the original long vowel remains long.

The "short vowel" verbs, however, must follow a different spelling method. Remember that a "short vowel" word ends in a V–C sequence. It might also end with V–C–C, like *staff* and *back*, or the V–C–C sequence might be found in the middle of a word, like *buckle*. Wherever the vowel appears, if it heads a V–C or V–C–C combination, it is usually short. But suppose we added *-ed* or *-ing* to a V–C verb like *hop*. We would get a V–C–V sequence (*hoping*), which would change the vowel to a long sound (and, in this case, also change the meaning of the verb). To prevent this unwanted change, we have to follow the familiar "double the final consonant" rule. This doubling gives the proper V–C–C sequence, thus keeping the vowel short. All of which explains the difference between *hop, hopped, hopping* (V–C or V–C–C, the short-vowel sequence) and *hope, hoped, hoping* (V–C–V, the long-vowel sequence).

This rule about doubling the final consonant to retain the short vowel, however, applies only when the accent falls on the short-vowel syllable. If another syllable is accented, the final consonant need not be doubled, for the short vowel stays short anyway. And <u>this</u> explains the difference between *repél, re-pélled* and *rével, réveled.* Sometimes, too, the accent shifts when a verb takes an ending that converts it to a noun; so though *occúr* needs a doubled consonant when it changes to *occúrrence, refér* shifts its accent and doesn't double to make *réference.*

Finally, we must consider the *c* and *g* variations. Both these consonants have two sounds, the "hard" sounds that can be labeled "k" and "g" and the "soft" sounds labeled "s" and "j." The "k" and "g" sounds occur before *a, o,* and *u,* as in *cat, cot, cut* and *gat, got gut.* The "s" and "j" sounds occur before *e, i,* and *y: cent, city, cytoplasm* and *gem, gin, gym.* (*Get* is an obvious exception here, just as *come* is an exception to the "long vowel, silent *e*" rule. But exceptions like these are such common, simple words that they cause no problems.)

Verbs ending in soft *c* or *g* sounds always have a final silent *e* to ensure softness; a "hard *c*" word often tacks on a *k* (as in *tack*) to emphasize hardness. Adding *-ed* or *-ing* to such verbs doesn't change the sound, for you still have an *e* or an *i* following the soft consonants, and you have the *k* to protect the hard *c* from the vowels. A verb like *picnic,* however, has to add a *k* in the past and participial forms to keep its *c* a hard sound: *picnicked* and *picnicking.*

Verbs ending in *ng* (*bring, clang*) appear to violate the rule, for the *g* does not soften in *bringer* or *bringing.* Actually, though, the final consonant is not *g* but the nasal combination *ng* (a single consonant sound, symbolized in many dictionaries by ŋ), a sound that is not affected by a subsequent vowel. One verb of interest here is *singe,* with the soft *g* sound and a silent *e.* Its present participle form is *singeing;* it must keep the silent *e,* partly to reinforce the soft sound, partly to distinguish it from *singing.*

Again, when suffixes are attached to verbs to convert them into other parts of speech like nouns and adjectives, the concept of hard and soft sounds affects the spellings. Thus, though the silent *e* is normally dropped before an *-able* or an *-ous* (*note, notable; blaspheme, blasphemous*), it stays in *change, changeable* and *outrage, outrageous* to separate the soft *g* from the *a* or *o*.

English spelling has a bad image. We've seen some of the grammar-related spelling problems that can arise. Many other spelling rules and exceptions to the rules exist that we can't consider here. Your initial feeling may be that spelling is chaotic. Yet, if you look over this chapter once again, you should note more regularity than spelling is usually given credit for. There <u>are</u> certain pockets of rationality amid the confusion. The chaos is only partial, not total.

Some lucky people have an inborn knack for spelling. Most of us don't. Some of us unlucky ones shrug off our faults by claiming that proper spelling doesn't really matter. If this is your excuse, forget it. Spelling does matter, both in the clarity and ease of reading it promotes and in the personal impression it makes on your reader. If you have serious problems, study a spelling book. If you have isolated problems—and we almost all have our pet spelling demons—first, remember what those few problem words are and, second, remember to consult a dictionary whenever you need to write them. Or if you really want to save time, you might even learn to spell them yourself.

34

A Writer's Bookshelf

This book assumes that you need to write in order to succeed in your work. If you have read this far, the assumption is probably true. And if it is true, you are no doubt willing to back up that need with an investment in other books that can guide and advise you. Every writer ought to have a home reference library of writing aids. As a basic investment, you might want to start with these five types of reference books.

1. A current dictionary to check spellings and word definitions. A good dictionary can also give you clues about a word's connotations, its "aura" and vibrations. The dictionary should be at least a college-level edition, published within the last decade. I recommend *The American Heritage Dictionary of the American Language, Second Edition* (1982).

2. A thesaurus for locating synonyms. Warning: Always check a thesaurus entry in your dictionary before using it, to be sure its meaning and its connotations fit your needs. *Stubborn, obdurate, pigheaded, tenacious, mulish,* and *resolute* may all be listed in a thesaurus as synonyms of *obstinate,* but they are scarcely interchangeable. I recommend any recent edition of an unabridged Roget's or Charlton Laird's *Webster's New World Thesaurus* (1971).

3. A usage dictionary for questions of acceptability and appropriateness. Usage dictionaries discuss an amazing range of language problems, from minor quibbles to major distinctions. They are also indispensable for settling bar bets. I recommend Bergen Evans and Cornelia Evans's *Dictionary of Contemporary American Usage* (Random House, 1957). It's a trifle old, but excellent. For more up-to-date advice, try William Morris and Mary Morris's *Harper Dictionary of Contemporary Usage* (1975).

4. A complete handbook of mechanics for questions of punctuation, spelling, capitalization, abbreviations, and many other details. These are sometimes called *stylebooks,* though "style" here is not the style that we have been discussing. Many organizations have their own "house style," and some professions or disciplines have idiosyncratic styles. Should this be true of your field, you will need the specialized guidelines. But you may also want a fuller, general handbook. I recommend *The Chicago Manual of Style,* 13th edition (1982) or *Words into Type* (Prentice-Hall, Inc., 1974). For less money, you can get the *Washington Post Desk Book on Style* (McGraw-Hill, 1978). It is not as complete, but it's handier.

5. A handbook on writing documented papers, particularly for academic writers. These handbooks illustrate footnote and bibliographic forms for a variety of source materials, in addition to giving general advice on how to prepare a lengthy research paper. I recommend either William Giles Campbell and Stephen Vaughan Ballou's *Form and Style: Theses, Reports, Term Papers* (Houghton Mifflin, 1978) or Kate L. Turabian's *Manual for Writers of Term Papers, Theses, and Dissertations* (University of Chicago, 1973).

As a final suggestion, since the grammar discussions in this book are selective and incomplete, you may wish to own a more structured and detailed grammar for situations not touched upon here. Unfortunately, few good grammars for general reference are available. Most adult grammars are either basic exercise-filled texts or advanced studies built on scholarly and unfamiliar language models like transformational grammar. Your best bet probably is George Curme's *English Grammar,* an old dependable published in paperback by Barnes and Noble. Curme presents a thorough, fact-filled digest of traditional grammar. It's not easy reading, but it <u>is</u> well indexed.

Many other books on the market offer advice to volunteer or conscript writers. One type that you may wish to purchase is a guide to improved writing style. You will find a wide choice. No one book is outstanding in this area; many books are useful. So examine the tables of contents, browse through the pages, and take your pick. Remember that a cheap paperback may be just as helpful as an expensive volume.

Get in the habit of dipping into all these books. Familiarize yourself with the subject matter and organization of each and with the particular kinds of problems each one tackles. These reference books can prove quite instructive and comforting. What's more, some of them are just plain fun.

VIII

Epilogue

35

What Next?

You know how to construct and punctuate a good grammatical sentence. You know how to string two or three sentences together with clear grammatical links and logical relations. So what do you do now?

You write. At this point, as far as this book is concerned, you are on your own. But since we have already breached the grammar boundaries and dabbled a bit in style, we might as well close with a few glances at the two triads that govern the whole writing process.

Briefly, writing takes place in three recursive stages—thinking, writing, and revising, the first triad. You fiddle around thinking about what you want (or need) to write. Then you write. Then you think some more. Then you revise what you have written. Then you write some more, revise again, think again, finish writing, finish revising—and, with luck, finish needing to think about that particular piece of prose.

As you are weaving in and out among these three activities—thinking, writing, and revising—you need to keep three considerations constantly in mind: your subject, your audience, and your purpose, the second triad. What subject are you writing about? What readers are you writing for? Why are you writing about this subject for these readers; what do you hope to prove? Your answers to these questions will guide every writing decision you will have to make.

If your subject matter is quite technical, for example, and if you are writing to colleagues in your field for the purpose of informing them of new research, you will probably not need to define elementary terms or clarify your ideas with a raft of examples. The expert audience will be able to understand you, even if you jump right into the new discoveries with a minimum of explanation. But if you are discussing the same research for an audience of laymen in order to convince them of the importance of the work, you will need lots of definitions, illustrations, and analogies to help them grasp your ideas. Or again, if you are writing for your fellow workers, your tone might be somewhat informal. If you are trying to impress faceless authorities, you would aim at a more formal and respectful tone. And if your audience is faceless but friendly—the well-known "common reader"—you might adopt a tone of ease and intimacy, but only if ease and intimacy are appropriate to your subject and your purpose.

So as you move about in the process of thinking, writing, and revising, always bear in mind your subject, your audience, and your purpose. With this pair of triads to guide you, with your newly burnished understanding of written grammar, with your own instinctive sense of the English language, you are in business. Good luck!

Index

Q

Jane Walpole, a teacher of English composition, realized when lecturing to lawyers that many of them were shaky in grammar. She reasoned that if lawyers need help with grammar, so must many other educated adults. *The Writer's Grammar Guide* was written in response to this need.